Buying and Selling Art and Collectibles

A LEGAL GUIDE

Armen R. Vartian and
Laura C. Tiemstra

ABA
AMERICAN BAR ASSOCIATION
Solo, Small Firm and
General Practice Division

Cover design by Jill Tedhams/ABA Design

Printed in the United States of America.

26 25 24 23 22 5 4 3 2 1

Library of Congress Cataloging-in-Publication Data

Names: Vartian, Armen R., author. | Tiemstra, Laura C., author. | American Bar Association. Solo, Small Firm and General Practice Division
Title: Buying and selling art and collectibles : a legal guide / Armen Vartian and Laura Tiemstra.
Description: Chicago, Illinois : American Bar Association, [2021] | Includes index. | Summary: "Buying art and collectibles is a passion for Americans. From the imposing sales rooms at Sotheby's to the local swap meet, we all search for objects that are interesting or will increase in value over time (hopefully, both). But few of us know where to go to learn our legal rights and remedies when buying or selling art and collectibles. For example, what if a work of art turns out to be a fake? Or a "rare" stamp or coin isn't as rare as the dealer said? When buying or selling through auction houses, can you negotiate the commission and other terms? Are insurance and other expenses related to art or collectibles tax deductible? This book answers those questions and many, many others, and gives the reader a good working knowledge of legal aspects of buying and selling art and collectibles"--Provided by publisher.
Identifiers: LCCN 2021057137 (print) | LCCN 2021057138 (ebook) | ISBN 9781639050826 (paperback) | ISBN 9781639050833 (epub)
Subjects: LCSH: Retail trade--Law and legislation--United States. | Sales--United States. | Selling--Art--United States. | Selling--Collectibles--United States. | Law and art--United States.
Classification: LCC KF2005 .V37 2021 (print) | LCC KF2005 (ebook) | DDC 344.73/097--dc23/eng/20220202
LC record available at https://lccn.loc.gov/2021057137
LC ebook record available at https://lccn.loc.gov/2021057138

Discounts are available for books ordered in bulk. Special consideration is given to state bars, CLE programs, and other bar-related organizations. Inquire at Book Publishing, ABA Publishing, American Bar Association, 321 N. Clark Street, Chicago, Illinois 60654-7598.

www.shopABA.org

Contents

Acknowledgments vii
About the Authors ix
Introduction xi

Part 1 Buying and Selling Art and Collectibles through Dealers 1

Chapter 1
The Written Contract 3

Chapter 2
Express and Implied Warranties Generally 9

Chapter 3
Warranties of Authenticity, Condition, and Rarity 23

Chapter 4
Getting Good Title 43

Chapter 5
Buying Art and Collectibles for Investment 51

Chapter 6
Selling Art or Collectibles through Dealers 71

Chapter 7
Miscellaneous Aspects of Buying Art or Collectibles 79

PART 2 Buying and Selling Art and Collectibles at Auction 83

Chapter 8
Consigning to Auction 85

Chapter 9
Buying at Public Auction 101

PART 3 Buying and Selling Art and Collectibles Remotely 113

Chapter 10
Basics of Buying and Selling Collectibles Online 115

Chapter 11
Copyright Considerations When Displaying Art and Collectibles Online 125

Chapter 12
Telemarketing 137

Chapter 13
Additional Rights and Risks When Buying or Selling Remotely 143

PART 4 Additional Considerations Unique to Certain Art and Collectibles 151

Chapter 14
Illegal Art or Collectibles 153

Chapter 15
Buying and Importing Cultural Property 157

PART 5 Dispute Resolution in Art and Collectibles Transactions 165

Chapter 16
Negotiation, Arbitration, and Litigation 167

Chapter 17
The Federal Trade Commission and Other
Government Agencies 179

PART 6 Taxation of Art and Collectibles **185**

Chapter 18
Sales, Use, and Income Taxes 187

Index 201

Acknowledgments

I would like to give thanks to my clients for giving me such interesting and challenging work over the past forty years and encouraging me to write a book about it. I have been privileged to have a career working with people who share my love of history, and who recognize the unique power of art and collectibles to educate as well as provide pleasure and profit.

Thanks to Laura Tiemstra, for over ten years of enjoyable collaboration as my research assistant, associate, partner, and now co-author.

Thanks also to the kind and helpful people who shepherded this book through publication, especially Lorraine Murray at the American Bar Association and Lynn Gohn at Progressive Publishing Services.

And thanks most of all to my wife Candice, and my sons Greg and Eliot, whose love and support mean everything to me.

Armen Vartian

Thanks to Armen, for sharing his years of wisdom and experience in this unique and fascinating area of law.

And thank you to our clients, for sharing their expertise in art and collectibles as well as the opportunity to take part in protecting and building their business ventures and/or collections.

Laura Tiemstra

About the Authors

Armen R. Vartian founded the Law Offices of Armen R. Vartian in 1991; the law firm concentrates in the areas of art and collectibles law, and has represented dealers, auction houses, collectors, investors, museums, artists, and institutions from throughout the United States and abroad. Mr. Vartian contributed a bimonthly column discussing legal considerations in the numismatic publication *Coin World* for more than twenty years, and also was a contributor of articles about the luxury art and collectibles markets for *Fortune China*. Mr. Vartian is a vice chair of the Art & Cultural Heritage Law Committee, a section of the ABA International Law Section, and is an editor and frequent contributor to the Committee's Newsletter. Mr. Vartian graduated from Brooklyn College of the City University of New York in 1978 and Harvard Law School in 1981. Mr. Vartian is a member of the New York, Illinois, and California bars, and has been working in the art and collectibles industry since 1984.

Laura C. Tiemstra is a partner in the Law Offices of Armen R. Vartian, a law firm that concentrates in the areas of art and collectibles law, and has represented auction houses, grading services, and individual collectors. Ms. Tiemstra is an editor and contributor to the Art & Cultural Heritage Law Committee's Newsletter, a section of the ABA International Law Section. Ms. Tiemstra graduated from Boston University in 2009 and Indiana University Maurer School of Law in 2012. She is a member of the Illinois and California bars and has been working in the art and collectibles industry since 2012.

Introduction

Buying art and collectibles is a passion for Americans. From the imposing sales rooms at Sotheby's to the local swap meet, we all search for objects that are interesting or will increase in value over time (hopefully, both). Billions of dollars are spent every year, and the numbers are increasing. But few of us know where to go to learn our legal rights and remedies when buying or selling art and collectibles. For example, what if a work of art turns out to be a fake? Or a "rare" stamp or coin isn't as rare as the dealer said? When buying or selling through auction houses, can you negotiate the commission and other terms? Are insurance and other expenses related to art or collectibles tax deductible? This book answers those questions and many, many others, and gives the reader a good working knowledge of legal aspects of buying and selling art and collectibles.

The book is divided into six parts. Part 1 relates to buying and selling art or collectible items through retail galleries or shops, including getting good title, warranties of grade and authenticity, and buying for investment. Part 2 relates to buying and selling at public auction, including contractual provisions in auction contracts and the mechanics of bidding at auction. Part 3 relates to online purchases and sales, and how those differ from retail and traditional auction transactions. Part 4 addresses certain types of art and collectibles that may be illegal to own or import into the United States. Part 5 covers resolution of disputes involving art and collectibles, from negotiating with dealers to suing in court. And Part 6 discusses the tax aspects of buying and selling art and collectibles, including sales and use tax, deductibility of insurance and other expenses, and other issues.

Whether you are a practicing attorney or a serious collector, we hope you will find this book useful as a general reference for whatever issues might come up for you relating to art and collectibles. But be warned: individual situations differ, and no single book can substitute for the advice of a competent attorney on a specific point. This book is not intended as your *only* source. Rather, we'd like you to think of this book as your *first* source. If you have a problem, read our general discussion here. Then, you'll know how to describe the problem for yourself or for an attorney you choose to hire, and what specific questions you'll need answered. We have specialized in this field for many years, more than thirty-five for Armen and more than nine for Laura. It is (almost) as enjoyable to do legal work involving such fascinating items as it is to collect the items themselves. Hopefully the knowledge you obtain from this book will make your experiences with art and collectibles more enjoyable as well.

PART 1

Buying and Selling Art and Collectibles through Dealers

What happens if the Sung vase, Matisse print, or "Prince-played" guitar you bought a few months (or years) back turns out to be a fake? Or the uncirculated coin you bought turns out to be circulated? Is the dealer responsible? Whether there is a ten-page written agreement, a mouse click, or simply a handshake, the purchase of art or collectible items always constitutes a contract between a buyer and a seller. Chapter 1 explains what is commonly found in that contract and why written contracts are so important, and chapter 2 explains how key warranties and disclaimers allocate the risks of buying such items between buyers and sellers. Chapter 3 explains what warranties as to authenticity, condition, and rarity are included in a purchase and which must be expressly added in writing. Chapter 4 addresses securing good title. Chapter 5 explains considerations when purchasing art and collectibles for investment purposes. Chapter 6 addresses specifics unique to selling through dealers, and chapter 7 identifies additional considerations unique to buying or selling art or collectibles.

1

The Written Contract

Most people have heard to "get it in writing"—that is, make a written record of your purchase transactions. This is good advice generally when you are buying anything on the basis of what someone else tells you, particularly something expensive. But it is especially important when buying art or collectibles, for reasons explained throughout this chapter.

THE STATUTE OF FRAUDS

The most important reason for a written contract is a practical one. If there is an agreement, the parties should have something besides their own memories to rely upon in remembering the terms of that agreement. Even close friends know that agreements are stronger and more closely followed if they are in writing and unambiguous. But there is also a good legal reason to have a written agreement. Oral agreements to sell art or collectibles may not be enforceable against the other party, based on a very old principle of law called the Statute of Frauds. The Statute of Frauds, which is incorporated in most states' laws through Section 2-201 of the Uniform Commercial Code (UCC), declares that contracts for the sale of goods over five hundred dollars are not enforceable unless they are in writing and signed by the party to be charged with the obligation. The purpose of this rule is to avoid "your word against mine" litigation over exactly what oral agreements might have been made between buyers and sellers. The document need not be formal. The official comment to UCC § 2-201 states that "It may be written in lead pencil on a scratch pad," and summarizes the writing requirements as follows:

> First, it must evidence a contract for the sale of goods; second, it must be "signed," a word which includes any authentication which identifies the party to be charged; and third, it must specify a quantity.

CONTRACT = OFFER + ACCEPTANCE

Taking these individually, UCC § 2-201 requires that the writing "evidence a contract for the sale of goods," as opposed to an offer to negotiate a sale, or an offer to do something else. For example, consider a letter signed by John Smith stating "I'd like to buy your Mickey Mantle Topps rookie card for $175,000. Write me if you are interested." This is not a contract, but merely an offer. The recipient must *accept* the offer, by writing back something to the effect that "I accept your offer to buy my Mantle card for $175,000," or even "I accept the offer in your recent letter to me." Without an acceptance, Mr. Smith could withdraw the offer at any time and either buy the card from someone else or lower his prior offer. But an offer letter and acceptance letter, taken together, would constitute a writing satisfying the UCC, and both parties would be legally bound to complete the transaction.

Likewise, if the recipient had written back that "I'd be willing to let you have my Mantle card for 6 months for $5,000," there would not be a contract of sale, because the acceptance does not match Mr. Smith's offer, which was for a purchase only, not a loan.

THE SIGNATURE REQUIREMENT: WHO'S DOING BUSINESS WITH WHOM?

The second § 2-201 requirement is that the writing must be "signed," through some "authentication which identifies the party to be charged." There doesn't have to be an original signature, and in most commercial contracts neither party actually *signs* the written documents. However, the use of a dealer's invoice form, handwritten identification of the parties, or anything else clearly stating who is doing business with whom, will satisfy the UCC. In recent years, most states have enacted laws recognizing electronic signatures as the equivalent of handwritten ones, and at the federal level (where interstate or foreign commerce is involved), the ESIGN (Electronic Signatures in Global and National Commerce) Act, 15 U.S.C. § 7001, does the same.

We've all gotten used to applying electronic signatures on legal documents we sign, and there seems no chance we'll ever return to "wet" signatures for most types of agreements.

The "signing" requirement raises two other important things to keep in mind: (1) know exactly who you're dealing with and (2) try to have the other party draw up at least part of the agreement. Beyond stating the obvious, identifying the other party to the contract can be very important where the parties might be doing business either personally or through a corporation. Armen once represented a person who had a claim against an art gallery owned by Ms. X, and who always believed that the gallery owner was personally responsible for the debt because his contract was with "X Gallery," and Ms. X signed the contract. Ms. X, on the other hand, said her gallery was operated by a corporation whose name did not even resemble "X Gallery." Needless to say, by the time the case reached court, the corporate defendant had no assets, and Ms. X refused to pay. Proper identification of the parties would have solved the problem one way or another. Either Ms. X would have bound herself personally to the deal, or Armen's client would have been told that he was dealing with a corporation and might have thought twice about it. In addition, having at least part of the contract documents prepared on the other party's forms or stationery will help avoid a situation where the party denies having entered into the contract.

The "party to be charged" qualifying language is important. The UCC does not require that both parties have signed the document, but only the one who is denying the existence of the contract. If the non-signing party *wants* to perform the contract, the party who signed cannot refuse to perform on the basis that the party who wants to go ahead with the deal didn't sign. As will be seen in other contexts, an unsigned contract is voidable on the part of the non-signing party but is not void altogether. The defense only applies if the person who did not sign is the one trying to void the contract.

In 2012, New York State's intermediate appellate court interpreted a portion of New York's Statute of Frauds in a way that nearly turned New York's art auction business upside down. The case, *Jenack v.*

Rabizadeh,[1] involved the sale of a nineteenth-century Russian silver and enamel box for $400,000, the successful bidder's failure to pay, and the auction house's lawsuit to enforce what it alleged was the buyer's contractual obligations. New York's version of the Statute of Frauds, Gen. Obl. Law § 5-701(a)(6), requires auction houses to prepare "a memorandum specifying the nature and price of the property sold, the terms of the sale, the name of the purchaser, and the name of the person on whose account the sale was made." The auction house's "clerking sheets" referred to the consignor and buyer by number only. The court found that the statute was satisfied on the buyer's side, because the bidder form contained both the bidder's name and the same number listed on the clerking sheet, and was signed by the bidder. However, there was no comparable document identifying the consignor, as is customary in the auction business, where consignors typically maintain confidentiality from bidders and the public. The court refused to enforce the sale. New York's highest court, the Court of Appeals, reversed this decision based on the fact that the consignor's agent—the auction house—was identified by name and that was satisfactory under the statute. The court ordered the buyer to pay for the box, in the process stating clearly what the Statute of Frauds was—and was not—intended to do:

> The Statute of Frauds is designed to protect the parties and preserve the integrity of contractual agreements. It is meant "to guard against the peril of perjury; to prevent the enforcement of unfounded fraudulent claims."
>
> . . .
>
> The Statute of Frauds was not enacted to afford persons a means of evading just obligations; nor was it intended to supply a cloak of immunity to hedging litigants lacking integrity; nor was it adopted to enable defendants to interpose the Statute as a bar to a contract fairly, and admittedly, made . . .[2]

---

[1] Jenack v. Rabizadeh, 99 A.D.3d 270 (2012).

[2] Jenack v. Rabizadeh, 22 N.Y.3d 470, 476, 479 (2013) (citations omitted).

MUST INCLUDE QUANTITY; DOESN'T HAVE TO INCLUDE PRICE

The third § 2-201 requirement is that the contract must state a "quantity." With art and collectible items this is not a big issue, although it could be for the sale of bulk items such as silver bullion coins or sheets of postage stamps. The parties typically either sell a single item, or a group of items that are listed individually for purposes of the sale.

Note that the UCC does not require that the written documents contain the contract *price*. This seems odd, given the vital importance of price to any purchase or sale agreement. The UCC drafters' thinking, however, was that the court can insert a reasonable price into a contract using market information if the parties agree on what was sold but cannot agree on the price for it. However, because the court cannot tell the parties how *many* of a particular item should be bought and sold, an enforceable writing must include an agreed quantity.

ORAL AMENDMENTS TO WRITTEN AGREEMENTS

What happens when one or both parties to a written agreement make changes to that agreement orally? Do the amendments also have to be in writing? UCC § 2-209 says yes, applying the Statute of Frauds to oral amendments of any contract of sale, whether the original contract was oral or written. That UCC section also recognizes, and affirms, a common clause in written agreements, namely that they can be modified in writing only and not orally.

But there's a twist—subsection (4) of the section declares that "an attempt at modification or rescission" that doesn't satisfy the Statute of Frauds or violates a no-oral-amendment clause in a written agreement, may nevertheless "operate as a waiver." Here's an example. Suppose a gallery agrees to sell a painting and make delivery within seven days, and a written invoice is prepared and signed by both parties, the terms including a no-oral-modification clause. The next day, the gallery telephones and asks whether it can make delivery in fourteen days instead, and the buyer agrees. The painting arrives on the eleventh day, and the buyer refuses to accept it because it is "late." Even though the oral (telephone) modification would not satisfy either the Statute of Frauds or the express no-oral-modification clause, it will still operate as a waiver of the buyer's right to reject a delivery made eight to fourteen days after the contract.

EXCEPTIONS TO THE STATUTE OF FRAUDS

The Statute of Frauds is becoming less popular in the increasingly "paperless" business world of the twenty-first century. Over the years, the UCC has adopted certain "exceptions"—that is, situations where the existence of the contract can be proven without a written memorandum. The most common such situation is where the contract has been acknowledged by the parties' performance, such as where the seller has accepted payment for the goods and the goods have been accepted by the buyer. So, for example, an art dealer cannot deny the contract of sale for a painting if he delivers the painting to the buyer and cashes the buyer's check. However, keep in mind that without a written agreement, anything *else* that may have been agreed orally by the dealer—such as a return privilege or warranties regarding provenance and attribution—would be unenforceable because the oral agreements did not satisfy the UCC requirements.

SUMMARY

A written contract for the purchase of any art or collectible item should include the following:

- The name, address, and telephone number of the dealer.
- The date of the transaction.
- A full description of the item being sold.
- The price, including applicable taxes.
- The payment terms, if any.
- Shipment terms, if the item is being shipped.
- Any express warranties by the dealer (see chapters 2 and 3).
- Any disclaimers of implied warranties (see chapter 2).
- The dealer's repurchase policy, if there is one (see chapter 5).

2

Express and Implied Warranties Generally

Generally speaking, most legal problems arising from art and collectible transactions relate to whether items conform to the seller's description, with regard to their authenticity, type, quality, grade, rarity, or provenance. There are many traps here for the unwary buyer, and the key is to keep the risk of nonconformity on the seller, so that in the event of problems the buyer can demand a refund or other compensation. The most important way to do this is by getting warranties, which are assurances from the seller that the item is what it is represented to be. Warranties are absolute, meaning that the seller is responsible if the items do not conform, regardless of whether the seller *knew* they did not conform at the time of sale or was in any way negligent in describing the items. Because the risk of "honest mistakes" falls on the seller, breach of warranty is a very powerful legal tool for collectors and investors in art and collectibles.

As with the writing requirements, the Uniform Commercial Code (UCC) also is the source of most of the relevant legal rules and principles applicable to warranties. The remainder of this chapter will discuss express warranties, implied warranties, a dealer's ability to disclaim them, and the relevant statutes of limitations. Chapter 3 reviews specific warranties relating to art and collectibles.

EXPRESS WARRANTIES VERSUS STATEMENTS OF OPINION

Express warranties are those made in writing or orally at or before the sale, and which become part of the contract. They are the warranties the seller makes directly to the buyer, as opposed to warranties that are *implied* by the nature of the transaction or by indirect statements by the seller. Express warranties are personal to the specific buyer and seller, and ordinarily they do not extend to subsequent owners of the goods. In other words, if you purchase art or collectibles with a warranty from the seller, that seller will not owe any warranty to someone else to whom you sell the goods later (even one day later). Under UCC § 2-313, express warranties come in three categories: (1) affirmations of fact or promises relating to the goods, (2) descriptions of the goods, (3) a sample or model. If any of the above becomes "part of the basis for the bargain between buyer and seller," the seller is expressly warranting that the goods will conform.

Determining whether particular statements by a seller are warranties is sometimes tricky, and over the years certain interpretations have been imposed upon the UCC's language. For example, sellers are permitted to engage in "puffing"—that is, saying that the work they're selling is "the best" example of a particular artist or genre. Think of a dealer saying that an ancient coin, produced by hand-striking a hand-made die into a piece of metal, is "flawless." Obviously, this statement is not literally true, but it expresses a sort of opinion concerning the coin's unusual state of preservation. Learned Hand, a famous New York judge, called such boasts the "kind[ ] of talk which no sensible man takes seriously." And for the most part courts have been able to distinguish with common sense analyses whether statements by sellers are the sort that a buyer should reasonably rely upon when buying goods. Such a statement is considered a statement of opinion and not a warranty, meaning that the dealer will not have to back it up. Section 2-313 of the UCC defines statements of opinion as "an affirmation merely of the value of the goods or a statement purporting to be merely the seller's opinion or commendation of the goods."

In cases involving everything from used cars to bull calves, the courts have analyzed salespersons' pitches to determine whether particular statements became part of the purchase contract or were merely nonbinding opinions. Judges seem to look at whether statements are the type on which purchasers in particular markets reasonably rely in making purchases. Most people would agree that were they to buy a painting from a dealer who says it is "the best example I've ever seen from Picasso's 'blue period'" they would reasonably rely upon the fact that the painting is by Picasso, and perhaps that it dates from Picasso's "blue period," but not that it is "the best" from that period. However, in the rare coin market, a dealer's statement in writing that a particular coin is the "finest known" example of a particular date or variety would probably be binding on the dealer because that term is reasonably relied upon by rare coin buyers. Generally speaking, statements relating to the quality, rarity, or provenance of art or collectible items are far more likely to be considered warranties and not opinions if they are unequivocal, in writing, and made prior to the purchase.

In some states, such as New York and California, special state laws help buyers of certain types of art and collectibles by abolishing the distinction between opinion and warranty in purchases from dealers. In addition to the UCC provisions above, New York Arts and Cultural Affairs Law § 13.01 provides that when dealers in fine art multiples (including prints, photographs, and sculpture made in more than one copy) provide written "certificates of authenticity" or similar paperwork to their nondealer customers they expressly warrant all material facts contained in those documents. California Civil Code § 1744.7 does likewise. This means that factual statements contained in written documentation from a dealer covered by those statutes is much more likely to be deemed a warranty than an opinion. The statutes provide some small protection for dealers who act in good faith, however (see the section on "Authenticity" in chapter 3). With respect to the warranty-opinion issues, however, New York's § 13.01 specifically states that the "degree of warranty" given by a dealer in a certificate of authenticity is subject to the terminology used and the meaning accorded that terminology by the customs and usages of the trade at the time. We doubt that even under the New York statute a written statement that the Picasso was "the best I've ever seen" would be held against an art dealer. The primary difference between the New York and California statutes is, as will be seen below, that California's statute applies to more inexpensive works than does New York's. Both states, however, reacting to chronic abuses in the sale of autographed sports collectibles, adopted legislation barring the "opinion" defense in such sales. New York Arts and Cultural Affairs Law § 60.02 requires a written certificate of authenticity, including identifying information about the dealer as well as an express warranty relating to the autograph, and states that these express warranties

> shall not be negated or limited . . . because any statement relevant to the autographed collectible is, or purports to be, or is capable of being, merely the dealer's or the supplier's opinion.[1]

California's Civil Code § 1739.7 also requires dealers in autographed sports collectibles to give detailed certificates of authenticity containing express warranties that are not subject to an opinion defense.

But don't forget that despite the legislation I've just described, a vast array of collectible items are subject to no mandatory express warranty requirements at all. Therefore, it is up to the buyer to insist that the dealer "put it in writing," and in such a way that the dealer must stand behind the key attributes of the item he or she is selling.

IMPLIED WARRANTIES

The UCC recognizes that what a seller *doesn't* say is sometimes more important than what he or she says in inducing the buyer to make a purchase. Dealers convey certain understandings to buyers about their goods in other ways, and it would be unfair in some instances to hold dealers only to what they actually tell customers. Consequently, certain "implied" warranties are part of the sale of goods even where they aren't expressed in any oral or written agreement. Because these warranties create obligations for the dealer without express language, and collectors and investors might not even be aware they exist, anyone buying or selling art or collectibles should read this section carefully to understand their rights and obligations fully.

The most important implied warranty is the warranty of merchantability. UCC § 2-314(2) states that "merchantability" includes "pass[ing] without objection in the trade under the contract description," being "fit for the ordinary purposes for which such goods are used" and "conform[ing] to the promises or affirmations of fact made on the container or label if any." As discussed, New York and California have taken all ambiguity out

---

[1] New York Arts and Cultural Affairs Law § 60.02.

of the sale of certain art and collectible items, but in most cases the dealer need not make any express warranties at all.

Some years ago, Armen attended a collectibles convention and saw a Matisse print being offered for sale. But the dealer did not actually *say* it was a Matisse. It was in Matisse's style and bore Matisse's signature, but the print was marked only with a price and no other description. Armen also saw many baseball cards that certainly looked to be authentic and in mint condition, but the dealer did not actually *say* that they were. Without some kind of warranty, a buyer might be unprotected against the risk that the print was fake or that the card was altered. This is where the implied warranty of merchantability comes in, giving buyers of art or collectible items legal rights if those items are determined to be fake, counterfeit, or otherwise not in accord with their description or appearance. In other words, even where a dealer has made no express warranties regarding authenticity, attribution, or quality, those types of warranties might be implied into the sale by virtue of the catchall category of "merchantability."

Moreover, UCC § 2-314(3) provides that additional implied warranties may arise from "course of dealing or usage of trade." That means that the usual practices of art and collectibles dealers in a particular area may be incorporated to some degree into all sales. Usages and practices are crucial to dealer-to-dealer trades, where only partial descriptions of items are sufficient for everyone to understand what is being sold. But they also play a role in retail transactions, because certain terms with specialized meanings in an art or collectibles area will bind the dealer not only to the specific words, but also to those words *as they are understood in the trade.*

A simple example from the rare coin field is the use of the terms "uncirculated" or "mint state." For numismatists, these designations apply to coins with less than a certain level of wear or scratches, such that its condition resembles that of a coin when it left the mint. Although different grading standards are employed within the general classification "uncirculated" or "mint state," dealers and experts generally agree on the difference between those coins and circulated coins. A coin sold by a dealer as "uncirculated" or "mint state" must conform not just with the dealer's *subjective* interpretation of that term, but with the *objective* understanding of the term among numismatists. In other words, a coin that was purchased directly from the mint but then handled carelessly by its owner might be "uncirculated" in a technical sense but would not pass the industry standards for an uncirculated or mint-state grade.

Another implied warranty is that of "fitness for particular purpose," which derives from UCC § 2-315. This applies where the seller knows that the goods are being bought for a particular purpose. Its application to art and collectibles is tenuous, at best. However, conceivably it could apply where a dealer sells a non-weatherproofed sculpture to someone planning to display it outdoors.

DISCLAIMING WARRANTIES

All warranties created by the UCC can be disclaimed by dealers, subject to the limitations described above for states such as New York and California. However, the disclaimers must conform to UCC requirements, which are strict. UCC § 2-316 provides guidelines for effectively disclaiming implied warranties.

The first guideline is that, where possible, disclaimers will be interpreted so that they are consistent with language in other relevant documents from the dealer that create warranties. This means that a disclaimer may not work if other portions of the dealer's marketing materials appear to create the very warranties the dealer is trying to disclaim. For example, if a dealer gives express warranties of authenticity on the front of the invoice, he cannot disclaim those same warranties on the back of the invoice. Buyers should try to avoid "fine print" disclaimers at the bottom of advertisements where the ad copy includes any statements that might be deemed express warranties.

The second guideline for disclaimers is that the warranty of merchantability is disclaimed only by (1) referring to it specifically in a conspicuous written disclaimer or (2) using terms such as "as is" which "calls the buyer's attention to the exclusion of warranties and makes plain that there is no implied warranty." The UCC specifically states that terms such as "seller disclaims all warranties, express and implied" will NOT disclaim the warranty of merchantability.

Many entirely reputable dealers place legalistic disclaimers in capital letters on their invoices, and the presence of disclaimers should not deter buyers from making purchases. In the sale of certified rare coins, sellers should use disclaimers such as the following:

> Dealer sells coins certified by PCGS [Professional Coin Grading Service] or NGC [Numismatic Guaranty Corporation]. Each of

> these coin grading services is recognized within the coin industry for its superior expertise, and each guarantees unequivocally that coins certified by it are authentic and unaltered. Dealer relies upon those guarantees in selling coins, and does not independently verify whether certified coins are authentic or unaltered. Accordingly, Dealer expressly disclaims any express or implied warranties otherwise attaching to the coins, including that the coins are merchantable.

As will be seen in chapter 9, auction houses have taken the disclaimer of warranties to their limits, and buyers who desire the protection of such warranties often prefer to buy through retail dealers and galleries.

New York and California's mandatory warranties for sale of prints, sculptures, and autographed sports memorabilia are subject to special restrictions on disclaimers. New York will not enforce disclaimers in sales of fine art unless they are conspicuous and "in words which would clearly and specifically apprise the buyer that the seller assumes no risk, liability or responsibility for the authenticity of the authorship of such work of fine art." The statute specifically negates attempted disclaimers where the work is later proven to be a counterfeit. For fine art and autographed sports collectibles, the New York and California laws state that express warranties cannot be "negated or limited" simply because a dealer did not intend that warranties be made.

Another way that dealers can escape implied warranties is to give the buyer a chance to inspect the goods before entering into the contract. If the buyer either inspects or refuses a reasonable opportunity to do so, defects that the buyer ought to have found upon inspection are waived. However, this exception has only a limited application to normal retail purchases of art and collectibles for two reasons: (1) a return privilege after purchase will not be deemed the equivalent of a *prepurchase* inspection; (2) the UCC states that "a nonprofessional buyer will be held to have assumed the risk only for such defects as a layman might be expected to observe." UCC § 2-316, Comment 8. This means that if the defect with a particular item was obvious to an average, *nonexpert* observer, a buyer who inspects the item prior to purchase accepts it with the defect and can't raise the defect later as grounds for rescinding the deal. Examples of defects that can be waived this way are mounting hinges on unused stamps, heavy scratches on rare coins, tears in baseball cards, and ink smears on lithographs. However, as will be seen, most warranty claims relating to art and collectibles do not arise out of such "obvious" defects. Warranties of authenticity, designation, or authorship usually survive despite pre-purchase inspections.

MUTUAL MISTAKE

A short word on cases of "mutual mistake," where a contract is entered into with both parties believing certain facts to be true which turn out to be false, causing one party to seek rescission of the contract. A classic example is *Sherwood v. Walker*,[2] one of the most famous legal cases in American history, if only because all law students study it in their introductory contract law class. Defendant agreed to sell a cow named "Rose 2d of Aberlone" to plaintiff for eighty dollars on the assumption that she was barren, the price reflecting her value as beef (a fertile cow being valued at $750–$1000 at the time). After the sale, the defendant seller suspected that she was pregnant, and refused to deliver her when the plaintiff arrived with the money. The Michigan Supreme Court sided with the defendant, saying there never was a contract for the sale of a fertile cow.

In the art and collectibles world, cases truly involving this principle are rare and difficult. Rare, because the preceding sections make it crystal clear that express and implied warranties govern most sales, putting the seller squarely at risk should anything pertaining to the goods being sold be proven untrue. Difficult, because the "all or nothing" consequences of rescinding sales are so stark—courts often struggle with imposing those consequences when neither party is at fault in any way. A great case in point is *ACA Galleries v. Kinney*.[3] ACA bought a painting from Kinney after inspecting it, and both parties believed it to be a genuine work by the artist Milton Avery. ACA paid the agreed price of $200,000, and then had the painting examined by the Milton & Sally Avery Arts Foundation,

---

[2] Sherwood v. Walker, 66 Mich. 568 (Mich. 1887).

[3] ACA Galleries v. Kinney, 928 F.Supp.2d 699 (S.D.N.Y. 2013), aff'd, 552 Fed. Appx. 24 (2d Cir. 2014).

which said the painting was a forgery. ACA sued for rescission under the mutual mistake doctrine,[4] and the federal courts rejected the claim, holding that "[T]he doctrine of mutual mistake 'may not be invoked by a party to avoid the consequences of its own negligence,'" and that a party to a contract bears the risk of mistakes when "he is aware, at the time the contract is made, that he has only limited knowledge with respect to the facts to which the mistake relates but treats his limited knowledge as sufficient." In such situations, the court said, "it is sometimes said that in a sense there is no mistake at all, but rather 'conscious ignorance.'"[5]

Buyers' windfalls, for example, people buying paintings at garage sales that turn out to be Warhols, receive significant publicity. Definitely the sellers didn't know what they had, but do they get to rescind when they learn of their mistakes? Usually, the answer is no, because where items are sold "as is," both parties know there are no representations being made about the merchandise, and sellers bear the risk of undervaluing their goods.[6]

---

[4] It's unclear why ACA did not sue for breach of warranty. Two possible reasons are: (1) ACA itself was a dealer and had inspected the work before purchase, possibly negating any claim that it relied solely on Kinney's warranties; (2) authentication by an artist's foundation sometimes greatly increases the value of an artwork, and Kinney might have been able to show that ACA accepted the risk of the foundation condemning the painting after the purchase to avoid paying Kinney the price an already authenticated painting would have commanded.

[5] *But see* Feigen v. Weil, discussed in chapter 6, where New York's state courts allowed rescission despite the fact that the plaintiff could have gotten a second opinion before the sale.

[6] An interesting case was that of the "flea market Renoir," which Martha Fuqua claimed to have purchased for seven dollars in 2009 at a West Virginia flea market, telling her story to the national media after putting the painting up for auction. Unfortunately for her, the publicity led to her brother telling reporters that the painting had been in their mother's home for decades, and the *Washington Post* eventually uncovering the fact that it had been stolen from the Baltimore Museum of Art in 1951. A court ordered Fuqua to return the painting to the BMA.

STATUTES OF LIMITATION ON BREACH OF WARRANTY CLAIMS

Warranties don't last forever, and they shouldn't. In most cases the facts warranted by dealers about a product are either true or false as of the date of sale, and diligent buyers discover any discrepancies within a reasonable period of time. In addition, the UCC's express and implied warranty provisions force dealers to maintain back-up documentation for their warranties—or remember what they did or did not say to particular customers—until they are absolutely sure they would not be sued, which is a burden. The absolute nature of UCC warranties—requiring full refunds regardless of whether the dealer was deceitful or even negligent—increases that burden. At some point, there needs to be closure. Accordingly, UCC § 2-725 gives buyers four years from the date of sale to bring suit for breach of any express or implied warranty created by the UCC.

This is a very important limitation on a buyer's rights under the UCC. Four years from the date of sale, a buyer loses his or her right to sue for breach of warranty. It does not matter when the buyer learns that there was a breach, and it often happens that defects are not discovered until the four-year period has already expired. The UCC provides no relief in these situations. In *Firestone & Parson v. Union League of Philadelphia,*[7] for example, an art dealer who had purchased a painting he believed to be by Albert Bierstadt was barred from suing the seller five years after the sale when it became widely held that the painting was by a far less-renowned artist and was worth only one tenth of what the owner had paid. However, it is sometimes the case that dealers will accept returns of inauthentic items regardless of how much time has passed, to avoid damage to their reputations or simply to "do the right thing." Indeed, Malletts, an antiques dealer in London, once discovered that a Russian gold dinner service it had sold a customer twenty years earlier was a fake, and refunded the customer's £1.5 million purchase price plus interest, fully aware that the buyer could no longer sue for a refund. Armen even represented the owner of a rare coin who received a refund *plus interest* for a counterfeit coin thirty-eight years after the purchase!

---

[7] Firestone & Parson v. Union League of Philadelphia, 833 F.2d 304 (3d Cir. 1987).

The only exception to the four-year UCC statute of limitations is for warranties that extend to "future performance," in which case the limitations period does not start running until the future event does (or does not) take place. This exception rarely applies to the sale of art or collectibles, but it is asserted occasionally by unhappy collectors. For example, Armen once represented a dealer in a breach of warranty case entitled *Hagen v. J.I. Corporation*,[8] where the plaintiff claimed that certain rare coins were not of the "grade or quality" warranted by Armen's client when she bought them. Plaintiff argued that because the coins were supposed to go up in value and didn't, she could sue seven years after the purchase. The court stated that if there were any warranties concerning grade or quality, they would have been breached at the time of sale, and "there was no 'performance' for plaintiffs to 'await.'" The claim was dismissed.

In the art world, a typical case is *Rosen v. Spanierman*,[9] in which plaintiffs purchased a painting in 1968 represented to be by John Singer Sargent, received periodic appraisals from the dealer, and in 1987 learned from Christie's that the painting was a fake. The court refused to apply the "future performance" exception, distinguishing between works of art and consumer goods:

> Paintings, unlike more commonplace consumer goods such as washing machines, or automobiles, generally are not bought based on how they 'function'". Upon this theory, the Painting could 'perform' only by being an authentic Sargent . . . plaintiffs argue that because the authenticity of a painting does not change over time, the warranty necessarily guaranteed the present *and future* existence of the Painting as an authentic Sargent. . . . Nevertheless, the Court declines to ignore the literal language of the statute requiring an *explicit* promise of future performance.
>
> . . .
>
> Undoubtedly, the statutory language of § 2-725(2) was intended for situations in which goods contain a latent defect at the time of purchase that does not cause the goods to break down until some later time. In such circumstances, the buyers cannot know of the

8 Hagen v. J.I. Corporation, Civ. 88-1328L (W.D.N.Y. Sept. 21, 1988).

9 Rosen v. Spanierman, 711 F.Supp. 749 (S.D.N.Y. 1989), aff'd, 894 F.2d 28 (2d Cir. 1990).

> breach until the product "misperforms". In the instant case the Painting failed to exist as a Sargent as much at the time of purchase as at the time the buyers discovered the Painting's true nature. Although plaintiffs were unaware of the Painting's faulty performance, the performance never changed.

However, in *Balog v. Center Art Gallery – Hawaii, Inc.*,[10] a Hawaii federal judge indicated that art and collectibles was precisely the type of item for which a warranty of authenticity involved future performance, criticizing decisions such as the one in Armen's coin case and *Rosen*:

> In the view of this court, far from being based on sound reasoning, these decisions flow from a too literalistic application of the Code which takes no cognizance of the unique problem presented by the application of the U.C.C. to artwork and other collectibles . . . [I]n the case of artwork which is certified authentic by an expert in the field or a merchant dealing in goods of that type, such a certificate of authenticity constitutes an explicit warranty of future performance sufficient to toll the U.C.C.'s statute of limitations.

If this rule were applied to art and collectibles cases, the warranty of authenticity would, in effect, last for as long as the buyer holds the goods. The Hawaii decision will likely be seen as an aberration, however. The "future performance" exception is intended to deal with warranties which, by their very nature, might not be satisfied within four years, for example, tires warranted to last for forty thousand miles. A car owner who drives infrequently will not travel forty thousand miles in four years, but the future performance exception ensures that the dealer will still be responsible legally if the tires fail before forty thousand miles.

The state laws of New York and California discussed above do not, for the most part, extend the limitations periods that would otherwise apply. The important thing to remember is that the UCC relieves buyers of art and collectibles of the need to thoroughly research their purchases ahead of time, by imposing upon the dealer the responsibility for any mistakes. However, once the sale is consummated, the buyer must take care to verify any material facts about the item before four years have elapsed, or risk losing his or her right to get legal satisfaction from the dealer.

---

[10] Balog v. Center Art Gallery – Hawaii, Inc., 745 F.Supp. 1556 (D. Haw. 1990).

SUMMARY

Warranties are one of the strongest protections of a buyer's rights to receive the item they believed they were buying. Keep the following in mind to understand how to maximize the protections of warranties and be aware of their limitations:

- Keep the risk of nonconformity, even "honest mistakes," on the seller.
- Express warranties (which should be written in the agreement) include representations of fact that are part of the basis for the bargain between the buyer and seller.
- Warranties are limited to *facts* about the goods and do not include statements of opinion by the seller about the goods, including the value of the goods.
- Some states have laws requiring sellers to provide express warranties of authenticity.
- Implied warranties require sellers to conform to industry standards when using jargon to describe the goods.
- Buyers have only four years from the date of sale to bring a claim for breach of a warranty, so the buyer must exercise diligence to discover any such breach.

3

Warranties of Authenticity, Condition, and Rarity

Now that we've discussed how express and implied warranties work generally, it's time to examine the specific warranties buyers should expect when buying art or collectibles, how they should be expressed, and their limitations.

WARRANTY OF AUTHENTICITY/ ATTRIBUTION

The key warranty on art and collectible items is that of authenticity, sometimes called the warranty of attribution when applied to works of fine art. By simply describing a painting as "Howard Behrens – *Venetian Brilliance* 1992," an art dealer makes several express warranties about the work:

- That it was painted by an artist named Howard Behrens;
- That it is the work entitled *Venetian Brilliance*; and
- That it was made (or at least published by Behrens) in the year 1992.

And selling a rare vinyl record as an "original" of Elvis's "Good Rockin' Tonight" tells buyers that the record was manufactured by the company that first recorded the hit song (Sun Records), and that it is not a bootleg copy or subsequent re-recording. Through express and implied warranties, dealers always assure collectors and investors about the authenticity of what they are getting, and authenticity probably is the only warranty applicable to all art and collectible transactions.

As has been seen, terms contained in warranties are entitled to their literal meaning as well as to whatever special meaning is attributed to them in a particular area of the art and collectibles business. The art trade, for example, has certain distinctions relating to attribution that have been adopted as law in New York:

> Language used in a certificate of authenticity or similar written instrument, stating that:
>
> **a.** The work is by a named author or has a named authorship, without any limiting words, means unequivocally, that the work is by such named author or has such named authorship;
>
> **b.** The work is "attributed to a named author" means a work of the period of the author, attributed to him, but not with certainty by him;
>
> **c.** The work is of the "school of a named author" means a work of the period of the author, by a pupil or close follower of the author, but not by the author.[1]

California has similar rules entitling buyers of fine art to rely upon statements made by dealers in certificates of authenticity or otherwise.

Such phrases as "original," "mint state uncirculated," and "actual" may constitute express warranties of authenticity with respect to different types of collectibles. Moreover, because authenticity is the primary element of "merchantability," it is implied regardless of what the dealer may say. Often, simply associating an artist or celebrity with a particular item is enough to imply a warranty that the artist created the work, or the celebrity owned or used the item. But don't rely on *implied* warranties of authenticity. If at all possible, warranties of authenticity should be express, and in writing.

Most art and collectibles dealers are honest and scrupulous in describing the goods they sell, but sometimes you'll need to insist on

[1] New York Consolidated Laws, Arts and Cultural Affairs Law (ACA) § 13.01(3).

a full, written description. For original art this means that the artist's name, the name of the work, the medium, and the date it was produced may appear on the invoice or on a document incorporated into the invoice. For rare coins, an authenticity description could include country name, denomination, date, mintmark, and variety. For stamps, Scott catalogue number, color, watermark, perforation, and cancellation may be part of a warranty of authenticity. Many collectible items require more elaborate descriptions because their value depends on particular attributes or associations. Those attributes or associations must be clearly stated as part of a warranty of authenticity. For example, Bob Dylan's 1963 album "The Freewheelin' Bob Dylan" is relatively easy to obtain at classic vinyl record stores. So when an auction house in California described a particular copy of the album with a minimum bid of five thousand dollars, its description of the item included an explanation:

> After Bob Dylan refused to appear on the Ed Sullivan Show because CBS censors would not allow him to perform "Talkin' John Birch Society", either he or CBS (there are conflicting stories) had several cuts including "Talkin' John Birch Society" deleted from his upcoming album. A few copies managed to escape with the "censored" songs. It is estimated that fewer than ten copies of the mono version of this album exist. It is perennially at the top of the list of the world's rarest record album.

The description is especially important in this case because—believe it or not—the "extra" tracks aren't even listed on the LP's label, much less on its outside cover (there are reliable ways to detect it, without actually tearing open the wrapper and playing the record).

In reviewing written warranties concerning authenticity and attribution, make sure they match whatever oral statements were made to you by the seller, and that they are unequivocal. Sometimes there is legitimate doubt about art or collectible items, as will be seen later in this chapter. But if the dealer tells you unequivocally that the boxing trunks you are buying were Muhammad Ali's, the invoice should not say they are "possibly," or "believed to be," Ali's. This is common sense—if a dealer will not put oral statements concerning authenticity in writing, you should think twice about the purchase. Collectors and investors are presumed to have less knowledge than the dealer regarding facts and technical distinctions relating to authenticity, and you are, therefore, entitled to rely upon the dealer's warranties of attribution and authenticity and can hold the dealer liable if an item turns out to be a fake. The corollary of that rule, of course, is that if you are an expert in a particular area, you may not be able to rely upon a dealer's warranty of authenticity. In certain fields such as US Colonial period coins, seasoned collectors are often better able to recognize counterfeits than some professional dealers. For such expert buyers, statements by the seller might not be "part of the basis of the bargain" and would not entitle the buyer to rescind the purchase.

As noted above, New York and California have led the nation in protecting purchasers of certain art and collectibles in their states. Specifically, New York requires dealers to give purchasers certificates of authenticity whenever they sell "visual art multiples," which is defined by New York Arts and Cultural Affairs Law § 11.01.20 as follows:

> [P]rints, photographs, positive or negative, sculpture and similar art objects produced in more than one copy and sold, offered for sale or consigned in, into or from this state for an amount in excess of one hundred dollars exclusive of any frame or in the case of sculpture, an amount in excess of fifteen hundred dollars. Pages or sheets taken from books and magazines and offered for sale or sold as visual art objects shall be included, but books and magazines are excluded.

California Civil Code §§ 1742 *et seq.* is similar, but applies to all fine art multiples regardless of price. Both states require dealers to make several disclosures in their certificates of authenticity, including (1) the artist's name; (2) if the name appears on the item, how it got there (i.e., did the artist sign it or at least authorize it to be put there?); (3) the process used to manufacture it (i.e., lithography, serigraphy, photographic process); (4) whether the artist was dead when the multiple was made; (5) certain specific information in the case of "limited editions," which will be discussed in chapter 3; (6) the date the multiple was made.

New York and California require certificates of authenticity to be given to customers at the customer's request, or in any event before the sale is consummated. This means that a prospective buyer can ask for a certificate of authenticity without committing in any way to the purchase, just to see what the dealer is going to be warranting. Once the price is agreed and the sale consummated, a certificate of authenticity must be given regardless of whether the buyer asked for one. Moreover, these states require dealers to post signs in their places of business that contain the following information:

> California law provides for the disclosure in writing of certain information concerning prints, photographs, and sculpture casts. This information is available to you, and you may request to receive it prior to purchase.
>
> Article fifteen of the New York Arts and Cultural Affairs Law provides for the disclosure in writing of certain information concerning prints, photographs and sculpture. This information is available to you in accordance with that law.

Special protections are given to remote buyers of multiples, presumably because it is not possible to inspect mail order items prior to purchase. Catalogues, advertisements, or other written material from dealers soliciting a direct sale of specific multiples must also include lengthy descriptions of the certificate of authenticity requirements for each state, and give buyers the right to return items within thirty days for a full refund if they are unhappy with anything contained in the certificate of authenticity.

California and New York also require certificates of authenticity for autographed sports memorabilia being offered at fifty dollars or more, which must include the dealer's name, address, and signature, as well as (1) a description of the collectible and the name of the sports personality who signed it; (2) the purchase price and date of sale, unless that information appears in a separate invoice; (3) an express warranty that the item is authentic; (4) whether the item is one of a limited edition and, if so, provide certain additional information (see chapter 3). The California statute, § 1739.7(b), has long required certain additional items not required in New York, including (1) whether the dealer is surety bonded or otherwise insured against errors and omissions and, if so, proof of bonding or insurance; (2) the last four digits of the dealer's resale certificate number (for California sales tax purposes); (3) whether the item was signed in the dealer's presence; and (4) whether the item was obtained or purchased from someone else and, if so, the name and address of that person. Until 2018, § 1739.7(b)'s requirements applied to all autographed collectibles, not just sports memorabilia, but complex amendments enacted that year focused on sports items, and on dealers rather than auction houses or online platforms.

Beyond New York and California, at least twelve other states require certificates of authenticity for art or collectible items, mostly fine art multiples. If certificates are given voluntarily, of course, the statements in them may be express warranties under most states' laws. New York and California's laws are the most stringent, and provide specific rules regarding such voluntary certificates of authenticity in the sale of fine art, imposing upon dealers who choose to make such statements the burden of having them construed as express warranties, rather than statements of opinion.

Attribution and authenticity issues sometimes become quite complicated, as dealers and consumers struggle in court over alleged breaches of warranties. Where one expert says that a work is genuine, and another disagrees, what are buyers and courts to do? The case of *Dawson v. G. Malina* illustrates the point.[2] Dawson purchased certain Chinese art objects from Malina, an art dealer, and for each object Malina stated the imperial dynastic period from which it dated. For example, a large ceramic vase was attributed to the Sung Dynasty (960–1279), and two jade sculptures were attributed to the period of Chien Lung's rule as emperor (1736–1795). Dawson later showed the works to various experts who doubted that these attributions were correct, but Malina obtained opinions supporting his position and refused to accept return of the items. As the judge described it, Dawson and Malina each contended that the other had the burden of proving him dead wrong:

> Dawson argues that unless it can be found that these works of art were unqualifiedly what defendants represented each of them to be, he is entitled to relief for breach of warranty.
>
> . . .
>
> [D]efendants maintain that unless Dawson has conclusively established by a preponderance of the evidence, that the representations made by them were in fact inaccurate, his claim for breach of warranty with respect to these pieces must fail.

---

[2] Dawson v. G. Malina, 463 F. Supp. 461 (S.D.N.Y. 1979).

The court adopted a standard more favorable to Malina (the dealer) than to Dawson. Noting that attributing works to a particular period of Chinese antiquity is an "inexact science" and "to a substantial extent a subjective judgment," the court determined that where there was a "reasonable basis in fact" for a representation at the time it is made, there is no breach of warranty.

What happens when a work that is universally believed to be authentic at the time of sale is later determined to be counterfeit or misattributed? This happens periodically with rare coins, and more and more often with fine art. An example was a Mary Cassatt painting purchased from Sotheby's in 1987, but which the Cassatt authentication committee (which didn't exist until 1990) declined to authenticate in 1994. Sotheby's refused to refund the purchase price, and after litigation, a confidential settlement was reached. If a warranty of authenticity is absolute, a seller should always have to take back inauthentic items, at least until the statute of limitations expires. The question is whether the warranty is breached just because scholarly interpretations of authenticity change with time. New York Arts and Cultural Affairs Law § 13.05 seems to say maybe, at least in some cases. For fine art multiples produced after 1900, and photographs produced after 1950, "the existence of a reasonable basis in fact for information warranted shall not be a defense to an action to enforce such warranty." So buyers of such works are protected. However, for pre-1900 prints or sculpture casts, or pre-1950 photographs, or any other forms of fine art or collectible item, a dealer with a reasonable basis in fact for stating that the work was authentic and properly attributed will prevail despite a change in scholarly opinion. California Civil Code § 1744.7 provides the same rule as New York's but is written in more direct terms:

> [W]ith respect to photographs and sculptures produced prior to 1950, and other multiples produced prior to 1900, as to information required by paragraphs (3), (4), (5) and (6) of subdivision (a) of Section 1744, the art dealer shall be deemed to have satisfied this section if a reasonable basis in fact existed for the information provided.

Where both parties act in good faith, the issue of changing interpretations is very difficult. Chapter 9 will discuss how auction houses deal with it head on in their terms and conditions of sale.

The importance of general opinion regarding authenticity means that experts who deny the authenticity of works can find themselves being sued by owners of those works who fear that their opinions decrease or destroy the market value of those works. Probably the most famous art-related litigation in history, *Hahn v. Duveen,*[3] related to whether a painting entitled *La Belle Ferronnière* had been painted by Leonardo da Vinci. Harry and Andrée Hahn had brought the painting to the United States in 1920, and had announced its sale to the Kansas City Art Gallery for $250,000. A New York newspaper sent a reporter to get a quote from Sir Joseph Nuveen, a world-famous art dealer, who looked at a photograph of the painting and replied that the Hahns' work was a copy of an original work hanging in the Louvre Museum in Paris. The buyer cancelled the sale, and the Hahns sued Duveen, alleging that his comment made the painting worthless. Despite Duveen's free speech arguments, and a parade of experts supporting both sides, the trial ended in a hung jury and a settlement payment by Duveen. More recently, an association of Jackson Pollock experts was sued by a dealer who contended that its refusal to certify a painting he wished to sell as a genuine Pollock caused Sotheby's and Christie's to refuse to handle the work. The case was dismissed on technical grounds, but the case illustrates the importance of experts in specific areas of the market.

Even where particular items are authentic in some respects, they may not be exactly as described. Probably the most peculiar example in the fine art area involved "Salvador Dali" lithographs. Apparently in his later years, Dali signed huge numbers of blank sheets. A gallery obtained thousands of these sheets, and persuaded relatives of Dali to "authorize" original Dali lithographs to be printed on them. The gallery then sold the lithographs to the public as genuine Dalis, relying upon the unquestionable fact that both the lithographs and the signatures were genuine.

The greatest abuses, however, have been in the area of sports collectibles. For example, sports figures occasionally use members of their staffs, and even autographing machines, to sign their names to multiples of sports cards and other memorabilia, resulting in autographs that are authorized, but not authentic. New York has attempted to fight the potential for deception in this area through recent amendments to the

---

[3] Hahn v. Duveen, 133 Misc. 871 (N.Y. Sup. Ct. 1929).

Arts and Cultural Affairs Law that prohibit dealers from selling autographed merchandise if they know or have reason to believe that it was signed "other than by the sports personality in his or her own hand," and by laws that require dealers in autographed sports merchandise to expressly warrant authenticity, and to post the following disclosure in a conspicuous place near the merchandise:

> SALE OF AUTOGRAPHED SPORTS MEMORABILIA AS REQUIRED BY LAW A DEALER WHO SELLS TO A CONSUMER ANY SPORTS MEMORABILIA DESCRIBED AS BEING PERSONALLY AUTOGRAPHED FOR TWENTY-FIVE DOLLARS OR MORE MUST PROVIDE A WRITTEN CERTIFICATE OF AUTHENTICITY AT THE TIME OF SALE.

California further protects buyers of autographed sports items by requiring dealers to disclose the following: (1) whether the item was autographed in the dealer's presence; (2) whether the item was obtained from a third party and, if so, the third party's name and address; and (3) whether the dealer is surety bonded or insured against errors and omissions, with proof. Note that these are disclosure requirements only. For example, dealers are not *required* to be bonded, but they are required to *disclose* whether or not they are, so potential customers can make informed decisions.

Other authenticity problems result from the fact that authentic items sometimes demand premiums based on their association with particular individuals or events. For example, certain autographed sports memorabilia are far more valuable if they were "game used"—that is, used by the athlete during his or her playing days. It occasionally happens that a particular item carries an authentic autograph but was not "game used" as described by the dealer. A sports memorabilia dealer once told Armen a story about a man who came to him with several baseball bats autographed by Roberto Clemente, the legendary Pittsburgh Pirates outfielder. He represented that the bats were "game used," but the dealer told him that he had doubts because the bats looked too pristine. The man took the bats away but returned with them the next day. This time, the bats were scuffed from having hit a few baseballs. In 2012, six people were convicted in Illinois of applying "wear and tear" to unused jerseys and selling them for hundreds of thousands of dollars as "game used."

Similar problems attach to "treasure coins" and other artifacts associated with famous shipwrecks, as well as rock and roll memorabilia such as the guitars supposedly played by George Harrison or Jimi Hendrix, which sell for large sums at auctions and guitar shows. There may be no way to establish authenticity conclusively in such cases. The coins might legitimately have been from the time of the shipwreck but not have been aboard, and Harrison or Hendrix might have owned guitars but not played them (it's customary to sell such instruments with pictures of them actually being played by the musician). The buyer's only protection is the dealer's express warranty.

It's important to remember that counterfeiting of items as US coins and postage stamps is prohibited by federal law, and it is actually a crime to sell counterfeits of such items. In addition, associations of collectibles dealers have ethical guidelines that essentially require members to guarantee authenticity. For example, a rare coin dealer who is a member of the Professional Numismatists Guild (PNG) is prohibited from knowingly selling a counterfeit coin, and PNG members will always accept returns of such items. In addition, chapter 14 will discuss remedies under the federal Lanham Act and the Hobby Protection Act for sale of counterfeit or "grey market" art or collectible items, and the peculiar dangers of buying art and collectible items online "sight unseen."

BLOCKCHAIN AND NON-FUNGIBLE TOKENS IN ART AND COLLECTIBLES

As we write this section in spring 2021, the impact of blockchain technology and non-fungible tokens (NFTs) on the art and collectibles marketplace is a very hot topic. Christie's sale of *Everydays: The First 5000 Days,* a piece of digital artwork by the artist known as Beeple with an accompanying NFT for $69 million in April 2021, and sales of sports collectibles and their NFTs for millions of dollars apiece, have gotten the collecting world's attention. Even the renowned Uffizi Gallery in Florence, Italy, has minted NFTs of Michelangelo works in its collection and sold them for six-figure sums, in part to help in the museum's recovery from prolonged closure during the COVID-19 pandemic. Some knowledge of blockchain and NFTs is valuable to anyone in today's art and collectibles marketplace.

So, what are NFTs, and why are they addressed in the discussion of "authenticity" in this book? Answering the second question first, NFTs are based on blockchain technology, the primary function of which is providing verifiable proof of transactions that take place either on the blockchain itself or in the outside world and recorded on the blockchain. Blockchain is a digital database, commonly referred to as a "ledger," on which data are recorded in "blocks" of code—as blockchain users add more blocks, the record increases in size and scope. To blockchain proponents, the primary advantage of blockchain technology is that it is decentralized, so data blocks exist and are linked to one another in the cloud. Anyone making entries will have those entries verified by copies of the ledger around the world seeking agreement between each other. Bitcoin and Ethereum are leading blockchain platforms, and each also provides access to cryptocurrency.

Here's how all of this works in practice when artwork by Beeple or a sports collectible, for example, is bought and sold as an NFT. Blockchain's verifiable proof of transactions enables anyone interested in purchasing such items to obtain information about those items, namely, who previously owned them, and what they are. Blockchain data isn't recorded in only one, or even one hundred, servers that could be hacked or shut down. It involves computer systems worldwide that can access the "blocks," coded descriptions of items, and transactions involving those items. The real value of blockchain in connection with the provenance and attribution elements of art and collectibles comes from the fact that a particular item's seller cannot change previously recorded information about that item. Blockchain proponents call this an "immutable ledger" of an item's provenance. The art and collectibles markets are notorious for their lack of transparency, and auction houses and dealers rarely identify their clients publicly. Once an item is registered on the blockchain, however, the registrant is identified (at least to whatever extent is required by the platform—known as a "wallet"—used by the registrant), and anyone researching the item following its registration will see subsequent transactions involving that item, or be able to inquire about such transactions.

NFTs add an additional element of collectability to the authenticity and provenance elements already present when physical items are registered to the blockchain. "Non-fungible" means unique, and

NFTS are just that—coded to the blockchain to be unique. Beeple's *Everydays* is a jpeg file, and anyone can physically cut and paste pictures of it onto their computers, just as they could with any such image (we're not talking about copyright here, just the physical ability to copy an image). But those copies of *Everydays* do not carry the unique code attached to the NFT version, meaning someone searching the blockchain would find that there were no transactions recorded to the blockchain involving the NFT of this work that led to you being its current owner. You have **a** version of *Everydays,* but not **the** version, the one that cost $69 million. But why is one version worth so much more than every other? Probably anyone reading this book knows the answer. Because it's unique—something nobody else can have. One observer described the value of NFTs as "bragging rights to prove ownership of an on-trend digital art or collectible." In this respect, NFTs are simply the latest type of collectible, using the technology of the 2020s to create what until now would be more boringly referred to as "limited editions."

So how do you create an NFT and sell it for tens of millions of dollars? Forget the tens of millions part. Most NFTs sell for little to nothing, even in the feverish atmosphere existing in the art world. And creating an NFT from a digital file is fraught with various fees, including a "gas fee" which euphemistically references the high energy use involved in blockchain and NFT activities, a factor that keeps many environmentally conscious artists and dealers out of this field entirely. As an example, and depending on the platform, the sale of a single NFT uses approximately the same energy as a US household does in several days. Then, as mentioned above, you will need to find a platform on which to register your work and create a wallet. The wallet has a "public address" and a "private key." These are sometimes analogized to a mailbox with a key. Third parties can deposit into your mailbox, but only you have the key to the mailbox to access and withdraw the contents. It is somewhat simple after that to "mint" your NFT by registering it to your selected platform. Potential buyers can find it and bid on it, and you accept the bid just as you would through a more typical online sales channel. Payment will be in cryptocurrency to your wallet. If all this interests you, by all means go ahead. But our advice is to maybe let these markets mature a bit more before diving in.

WARRANTIES OF CONDITION, QUALITY, GRADE

The true value of authentic collectible items can often vary enormously depending on their condition. An uncirculated coin, fully centered stamp, or mint sports card is usually worth far more than a circulated, off-center, or wrinkled example of such an item. Even rare vinyl record albums are differentiated according to a detailed set of grading standards. Far more than authenticity, however, condition is subjective. Experts can all agree that a coin is authentic, and then disagree as to its condition. In addition, each type of item has its own commonly used standards, interpretations, and terminology relating to condition. Buyers must understand what standards are applied with respect to that particular item, and what interpretations of those standards are commonly used by dealers of such items, because those standards and interpretations will limit your rights against the dealer.

Here is an example. If a dealer sells you a coin described as an 1893-S Morgan Silver Dollar in Extremely Fine condition, at least two express warranties are being made:

- The coin is an authentic 1893-S Morgan Dollar.
- The coin is in Extremely Fine condition.

Undoubtedly, most experts can agree as to whether, in fact, the date, mintmark, and type of the coin is correct. But is the coin in Extremely Fine condition? More importantly, will a buyer ever *know* whether it is or is not? In coin grading, subjectivity prevails. Even with uncirculated or "mint state" coins, where the Sheldon Scale purports to place all coins on a scale of 60 (barely uncirculated) to 70 (perfect), experts will differ, sometimes significantly, about how a particular coin is graded. A dealer once submitted the same group of coins to twenty top dealers for grading, and for practically every coin, the range of reported grades was 3 or more on the scale of 60 to 70. And some major dealers refuse even to apply the Sheldon Scale, preferring their own "adjectival" grades, such as "Extremely Fine" and "Brilliant Uncirculated." These terms don't have direct numerical equivalents.

Grading/condition controversies between dealers and collectors are uncommon with original works of art, but with rare coins, stamps, sports cards, and sports memorabilia they can be very difficult to resolve. Differing grading standards are employed by different dealers, and even those standards have been known to change over time. This confusing situation has frequently allowed unscrupulous dealers to mislead or deceive their customers. For example, in 1989 the Federal Trade Commission brought suit against a Florida rare coin dealer who advertised coins as priced "below wholesale." Interested buyers were shown the *Coin Dealer Newsletter* (CDN), a respected weekly price guide to dealer-to-dealer transactions in most types of rare coins. For each coin listed in the CDN, there were reported prices in all uncirculated grades, and this dealer's prices were below those listed in the CDN. How did he do it? By selling coins graded in accordance with a more liberal—less stringent—standard than was employed by the CDN. That meant that the coins the dealer called "MS-65s" would have been graded MS-62 or MS-63 by most other dealers. That meant that the value of the coins would be found not on the MS-65 line of the CDN, but with the MS-63s or MS-62s. Far from getting a bargain, the customers were actually paying double the true wholesale price of the coins.

Fortunately, today most rare coins can be graded by reputable third-party grading services such as Professional Coin Grading Service (PCGS) of Newport Beach, California, or Numismatic Guaranty Corporation (NGC) of Sarasota, Florida, who assign a grade and encase coins in tamper-evident plastic cases. The dealer can then warrant that a particular coin has been graded PCGS EF45 – Extremely Fine—a statement the truth of which can be proved objectively. But where the coins have not been third-party graded, confusion continues to reign among experts, and a buyer has only a slim chance of prevailing in a breach of warranty action based solely on grade.

But having said that third-party grading services protect coin collectors and investors from fraudulent sellers, remember that all grading services are not alike. PCGS and NGC are the "gold standard," and collectors should exercise extreme caution in purchasing coins graded by any other grading service. Basically, any significant coin that is graded by a lesser grading service probably has been rejected by PCGS and NGC, for reasons such as having been harshly cleaned or its original surfaces altered.

Sports memorabilia is another major area where subjective measures of condition prevail. At one time, California attempted to codify a definition of "mint condition" as follows:

> "Mint condition" means any collectible sold on the open market or in a private transaction that meets all of the following requirements:
>
> **A.** The item has never been circulated, used, or worn.
>
> **B.** The item exhibits little or no signs of aging or degradation caused by oxidation or exposure to sunlight as a result of its display.
>
> **C.** The item is otherwise free from creases, blemishes or marks.[4]

This definition certainly eliminates circulated, faded, and otherwise defective items from the definition of "mint." It did not, however, resolve many grading issues relating to sports cards and memorabilia, and it was still best to buy from dealers who expressly warranted condition, and whose grades were backed by third-party grading services such as Professional Sports Authenticators (PSA) of Newport Beach, California, or SGC of Boca Raton, Florida. Ultimately, California replaced the above definition of "mint condition" with the requirements concerning dealer warranties for autographed sports and entertainment memorabilia (discussed earlier),[5] which includes a significant portion of the memorabilia in both of those fields. California also requires dealers of autographed collectibles to disclose whether they are surety bonded or otherwise insured against errors and omissions, which is a comfort to some wary buyers.

WARRANTY OF RARITY/ SURVIVING MINTAGE

Part of the appeal of art and collectibles is their rarity, and market value is often based on actual or perceived rarity. But rarity is relative when it comes to art and collectible items. A McDonald's prepaid telephone card that is one of ten thousand issued is relatively "common," as is a fine art print from a series of ten thousand. But if "only" ten thousand

[4] California Civil Code § 1739.7 as of 1995.

[5] California Civil Code § 1739.7.

of a particular US coin or stamp were ever issued, it would be rare indeed. On the other hand, modern commemorative coins and stamps produced by the US or foreign governments in such numbers are not considered rare among dealers. Even the same items may be perceived as common by some people and rare by others. Such is the nature of the art and collectibles marketplace.

We will not attempt in this book to explain concepts of rarity for particular art or collectible items, which could itself be the topic of a book. It is certainly beyond the scope of this one. But warranties relating to the rarity of art and collectibles are very important, and buyers promised "rare" or "limited edition" items need to know what to look for and expect. Certain federal and state laws provide guidance. For example, the US Customs Service classifies only sculptures of twelve or fewer copies as "fine art" for purposes of duty-free entry into the United States. The Visual Artists' Rights Act, 17 U.S.C. § 106A, applies only to lithographs in editions of two hundred or fewer. And California has two code sections that define the term "limited edition" without using any particular numbers. California Civil Code § 1739.7(a)(6) defines "limited edition" autographed collectibles as any item meeting the following requirements:

A. A company has produced a specific quantity of a collectible and placed it on the open market.

B. The producer of the collectible has posted a notice, at its primary place of business, that it will provide any consumer, upon request, with a copy of a notice that states the exact number of a collectible produced in that series of limited editions.

C. The producer makes available, upon request of a consumer, evidence that the electronic encoding, films, molds, or plates used to create the collectible have been destroyed after the specified number of collectibles have been produced.

California Civil Code § 1740 defines limited edition fine art prints as:

> [F]ine art multiples produced from a master, all of which are the same image and bear numbers or other markings to denote the limited production thereof to a stated maximum number of multiples, or are otherwise held out as limited to a maximum number of multiples.

The definitions of "limited edition" just given will not be legally binding on a dealer selling other types of art or collectible items. However, every dealer's use of the term must be reasonable for the particular item and, where scarcity determines price, the dealer should give you an express warranty of some kind. As noted above, California and New York require express warranties for fine art prints and sculptures, but the extent of the warranty depends on the type of art and its age. For example, for limited edition works made after January 1, 1983, both the laws of both states require disclosure not only of how many signed or numbered impressions were made, but also how many prior editions, contemporary unsigned or unnumbered impressions, artist's proofs, and publisher's proofs were made, and a warranty "that no additional multiples of the same image, including proofs, have been produced in this or in any other limited edition." For works made between 1950 and 1982, neither state requires disclosures relating to prior editions, and California does not require an express warranty that no other multiples were made, and New York does not require disclosure of the number of "proofs" made. The disclosure requirements lessen with older works, such that for works prior to 1900, neither state requires that the dealer disclose, much less warrant, the number in the edition. And dealers may disclaim knowledge of certain information required by the statutes but must do so expressly and "categorically" in the place where disclosure would otherwise be required. Hence, in the words of California Civil Code § 1742(d): "the purchaser shall be enabled to judge the degree of uniqueness or scarcity of each multiple contained in the edition so offered."

We don't recommend paying a premium to buy any item classified as a limited edition without a specific written warranty of some kind from the seller regarding total number in the edition.

Another rarity issue is survivability. With respect to contemporary lithographs or "commemorative" plates, the maximum number of copies produced is easy to determine. Certain other collectibles, however, are rare not because they were *made* in small quantities, but because they *exist today* in small quantities. Such items as rare coins, stamps, and antiquities fall into this category. Mintage is often irrelevant in valuing such items, and the seller should give an express warranty as to *surviving* mintage. There are also "condition rarities"—that is, items that are rare only by virtue of their fine state of preservation. Many of a particular Barbie doll may exist, but only a few in their original, unopened box—likewise for Beanie Babies sporting their original tags, or unopened packages of 1980s video games (in April 2021, Heritage Auctions sold a factory-sealed Nintendo Super Mario Bros. game for $660,000—reportedly it had been a Christmas present in 1986 but was forgotten in a desk drawer). These are indeed "rare," but buyers who pay a premium for condition rarities are assuming the risk that the majority of other collectors in that genre will also recognize that they are worth more. A major problem with condition rarities, or with any collectible whose value depends on a low survival rate, is that often one cannot verify the survival figures, and new discoveries depress the market price tremendously. Among coins, an Egyptian dodechadrachm from 222 BC was sold for $200,000 when it was believed to be unique. Once a "hoard" of eighteen more was discovered, however, its value immediately dropped substantially. In investigating a Southern California rare coin investment firm, Armen saw the following language in the firm's salesmen scripts:

> [T]he population of this coin at this grade by PCGS is only __ meaning the amount of coins graded thus far at this grade by PCGS is only __. Meaning there are only __ in existence by PCGS at this grade and this is one of them.

This statement was deceptive. The salesmen did not mention that PCGS was just one of the two major grading services, that a large number of rare coins are held in private collections and are ungraded by any grading service, and that many less-valuable coins aren't certified because for those coins the cost of certifying them isn't worthwhile. The clear intent of this script was to gloss over the truth in order to suggest to the investor that the dealer was expressly warranting rarity. The key to purchasing limited edition items is to have a firm written warranty from the seller as to just how rare the item is, and according to a standard of rarity recognized in the particular industry.

SUMMARY

Remember that authenticity is the most common source of problems for buyers of art and collectibles, and keep the following principles in mind:

- Demand that dealers give you specific, written warranties relating to authenticity.
- Understand the jargon used in different collecting areas before you buy.

- When buying sports collectibles, ask to see the certificates of authenticity and other disclosures required by state consumer protection laws, and don't buy from dealers who don't comply.
- Be familiar with how condition affects the value of particular items, and look for items that have been graded or appraised by independent, third-party organizations rather than only by the dealer.
- When buying "limited edition" items, understand how that concept differs among different collecting areas, and before paying a premium for any rare item, be sure that the premium is justified by the *market's* definition of rarity.
- If an item is thought to be authentic at the time of sale, you will probably bear the risk that later changes in scholarly opinion will reduce the value of that item.

4

Getting Good Title

Nobody would buy a house without making sure the seller had legal title. Home buyers, through their attorneys or title insurance companies, do a title search—that is, a review of officially recorded documents to verify that the property is unencumbered and belongs to the person offering it for sale. With art and collectibles, unfortunately, often there are no official title documents to review. And because stolen or other items of questioned title may be off the market for years, disputes over title may lie dormant until the item resurfaces. This chapter explains the more common issues relating to title to art and collectibles, and how to protect yourself as either a buyer or a seller.

WARRANTIES OF TITLE

The Uniform Commercial Code (UCC) § 2-312 provides that

> (1) . . . [T]here is in a contract of sale a warranty by the seller that (a) the title conveyed shall be good, and its transfer rightful; and (b) the goods shall be delivered free from any security interest or other lien or encumbrance of which the buyer at the time of contracting has no knowledge.
>
> (2) A warranty under subsection (1) will be excluded or modified only by specific language or by circumstances which give the buyer reason to know that the person selling does not claim title in himself or that he is purporting to sell only such right or title as he or a third person may have.

The drafters of the UCC put it beautifully when they noted that this section "makes provision for a buyer's basic needs," namely "a good, clean title" given "in a rightful manner so that he will not be exposed to a lawsuit in order to protect it." In a nutshell, the UCC allows good faith buyers of art or collectibles to presume that the items they are buying either belong to the seller or may be sold by the seller without claim by anyone else.

The warranty of title is implied into every sale, meaning that it is part of the contract even if it is not mentioned either orally or in writing. However, a warranty of title can be disclaimed, although that is quite rare in the sale of art or collectibles (we'll see an example in chapter 9 on auctions).

The presumption of good title provided by § 2-312 is not an absolute guarantee that no third party will ever claim the goods. It is only a guarantee that if such a claim does arise, the buyer can claim back against the seller for breach of the warranty. Ideally, when a third party shows that a sculpture you purchased three years ago is rightfully his, you would turn over the sculpture and recover your entire purchase price (plus interest) from the dealer. The reality of warranties of title is not nearly so good, however. A warranty is only as strong as the person giving it, and many dealers simply cannot easily refund a customer's purchase price. Also, as we will see, UCC § 2-725 limits claims for breach of the warranty of title to four years from the date of sale, while title claims can arise long thereafter. So, when buying antiquities or other items that often have dubious origins, it is best to get extensive provenance information and, better yet, to do business only with the most reputable dealers in the field.

TITLE TO STOLEN ITEMS

It is an axiom of the US law that nobody can pass good title to stolen goods. The true owner of an item may always recover it from its current holder, no matter how many times the item changed hands in between. Some years ago, Armen represented a Southern California rare coin dealer who had an extremely rare US twenty-dollar gold piece stolen from an overnight courier shipment to a New York dealer. Several months after that incident, the client was offered *his* coin at a coin dealers' convention, and he traced it back through a chain of other dealers to a dealer in New York who had bought it over the counter from someone who was obviously not a collector and for half its value. The client can recover the coin from whoever possesses it. While people who buy stolen art and collectibles in good faith (having no reason to think they were stolen) can almost always claim their money back from the dealer who sold them the items, they never acquire good title, and they must surrender the goods to the true owner if a timely claim is made. In Armen's case, the coin had to be surrendered, and the dealers along the chain of possession each claimed their purchase price from the one before them. Without such a rule, victims of theft could not be adequately protected, because thieves could put stolen items out of reach by selling them to innocent purchasers.[1]

We deliberately used the words "timely claim" in the preceding paragraph. Most states have statutes of limitations governing claims for replevin—that is, recovery of stolen property, such as the three-year statute in New York. Often, stolen art and collectibles end up in private collections, out of public view for considerable periods of time, such as when a Chagall gouache that disappeared from the Guggenheim Museum in New York in 1965 reappeared in a private art collection in 1985. Moreover, for priceless works of art, a thief might well wait out the limitations period before selling the loot. This can result in injustices, and occasionally a statute of limitations is modified. For example, in many states a "discovery rule" suspends running of the limitations period until the victim locates the stolen item.

With a discovery rule, a three-year limitations period would not even begin until the true owner found the item and knew against whom to assert his or her claim. But fear of claims being brought decades after a theft led states to modify the modification, and require the true owner to prove that he or she exercised due diligence in looking for the items, barring which the claim would be denied. This is still the rule in

---

[1] The US rule does not apply in civil law countries, such as France, Germany, and elsewhere in Europe. In those places, the true owner can recover items only by proving that the person possessing them had reason to know that they had been stolen. So in our stolen twenty-dollar gold coin scenario, the dealer buying an extremely rare coin from a noncollector for half of its value would be deemed to have had reason to know the item was stolen, but probably not the person who eventually offered the coin back to Armen's client—the victim.

certain states, including Indiana, the site of *Autocephalous Greek Orthodox Church v. Goldberg Feldman Arts,*[2] a landmark case involving stolen Byzantine mosaics, which we'll discuss in the context of "cultural property" in chapter 15.

In art market states, the courts feared that placing the burden of proof of due diligence on the original owner encourages thefts, by making it easier for thieves to "cleanse" their crime by keeping stolen art away from the market for several years. In New York, the law is that an innocent purchaser of stolen art or collectibles will prevail only if he or she can prove that the true owner knew where the items were and unreasonably delayed in bringing suit. In California, the true owner will have three years to sue once he or she has discovered "the whereabouts" of the stolen work. And since Congress's enactment of the HEAR Act in 2016, for anyone asserting title to artwork taken by the Nazi regime or related entities during the period 1933–1945 the period is six years beginning upon actual knowledge of the facts surrounding the claim and the location of the artwork, regardless of which state's law would otherwise govern.

"VOIDABLE" TITLE TO CONSIGNED GOODS

The rules governing stolen property are logical and easy to understand. But what happens when the items aren't stolen, but someone claiming to be their owner says he or she was never paid in full for them? More than twenty years ago, Armen was involved as an expert witness in a nationally publicized court case involving a Western painting. The owner of the painting had consigned it to a dealer on condition that if the dealer could not sell it within a certain period of time, the dealer had to buy it at a mutually agreed price. The dealer tendered a check for that amount and, when the time period expired, the owner deposited the check. The check bounced. The owner telephoned the dealer and discovered that the dealer had already resold the painting (for a fair price) to an art collector who was unaware of the bounced check. The dealer was broke, so the owner sued the collector for return of the painting.

---

[2] Autocephalous Ch. v. Goldberg Feldman Arts, 917 F.2d 278 (7th Cir. 1990).

The collector got to keep the painting. This is a clear example of what lawyers call "voidable title." Think of it this way—should the collector pay for the consequences of the dealer's bad check? In law, the bounced check will not impair the dealer's power to convey good title to the collector, for two reasons.

First, the check bounced after the sale, and after title had already passed. If the sale of a work of art could be rescinded because a seller has not yet paid the consignor, it would mean the end of the great public auction houses, who convey title to hundreds of millions of dollars of artwork each year but may pay their consignors as much as thirty to forty-five days after they themselves are paid. Bidders at a Sotheby's, Christie's or Heritage auction would be reluctant to risk their money if a subsequent payment dispute between the auction house and the consignor could result in their having to return the artwork. A bounced check from a dealer is a risk assumed by someone who wishes the benefits of consigning to a dealer, and as we'll see in chapter 6, that risk can be mitigated by working with a financially secure dealer or making appropriate security arrangements. Even dealers selling works consigned by the original artists have the power to convey good title to good faith purchasers regardless of whether the dealer subsequently pays the artists, despite the fact that in many states, dealers hold such works in trust for the artist by statute. In the case of the Western painting, the original owner assumed the risk that the dealer would transfer title before meeting all the payment terms of their consignment agreement.

Second, even if the dealer's check had bounced *before* the collector bought the painting, the collector was not aware of that fact and there was no reason for the collector to suspect that the dealer was not the authorized seller of the painting. There is a crucial distinction between "void" and "voidable" title. We have seen that had the painting been stolen from its owner the dealer would have had void title and could convey nothing to the collector or anyone else. However, the dealer did not steal the painting. The owner gave him the painting and authorized him to sell it. Therefore, at a minimum the dealer had voidable title. The UCC specifically deals with this type of situation in UCC § 2-403(1)(b), which states that the owner of goods who "entrusts" those goods to "a merchant who deals in goods of that kind" cannot challenge a good faith purchaser of the item from that merchant "even though . . . the delivery [to the merchant] was in exchange for a check which is later dishonored." The collector acted in good faith and without knowledge that the sale to him was in violation of the rights of the owner or any third party. He bought the painting for a fair market price from a recognized art dealer. This is an everyday commercial transaction, the type the UCC intends to facilitate with its protection of good faith purchasers. As the New York Court of Appeals stated in the case of *Porter v. Wertz,*[3] a case involving consignment of a Utrillo painting:

> The "entruster provision" of the Uniform Commercial Code is designed to enhance the reliability of commercial sales by merchants (who deal with the kind of goods sold on a regular basis) while shifting the risk of loss through fraudulent transfer to the owner of the goods, who can select the merchant to whom he entrusts his property.

In a more recent case, *Galin v. Hamada,*[4] the US Court of Appeals for the Second Circuit noted that "[T]his may be a bitter pill [to swallow]" for the aggrieved artwork owner, but the UCC provision "represents the most prudent allocation of risk." It is important to note under what circumstances a buyer of art or collectibles is not an "innocent," or "good faith" purchaser entitled to the protection of the "entruster rule." In *Porter,* for example, the dealer purchased the Utrillo from someone he had no basis to believe was an art dealer (he was, in fact, a delicatessen employee acquainted with a dealer who had obtained the painting by tricking its true owner—the telephone number he gave the dealer was to the deli but the dealer never checked it). And in a different case a dealer purchased a Grant Wood drawing for $205,000 from another dealer even though the owners of the drawing had told him personally that they wouldn't accept less than $400,000 for it.

Dealer invoices often contain the phrase "title does not pass until paid in full." Not only are these words meaningless in the context of UCC § 2-403, but Official Comments to that section specifically say so. I'm often surprised at how many long-time professional art or collectibles dealers think that they can recover consigned items from innocent buyers just because of a bad check from their direct customer. The UCC drafters, on the other hand, were focused on furthering commerce, and so in most

---

[3] Porter v. Wertz, 53 N.Y.2d 696 (1981).

[4] Galin v. Hamada, No. 17-2988 (2d Cir. Oct. 4, 2018).

cases, where an item is bought from a dealer at a fair price by someone who has no knowledge of any issues with that dealer, the buyer gets to keep the artwork and the original owner's remedy is against the dealer only.

PROVENANCE REPRESENTATIONS

Reputable dealers of art and collectibles know that buyers want good title and, whenever possible, dealers will research the provenance of unique or unusual items and provide the results of that research to the buyer at the time of sale. You'll recall from the previous chapter that for some items, the provenance is everything, because the value is entirely in the item's association with a particular person or event. Provenance is also quite important in verifying title, because an item that was held in a major collection for decades, or traded openly among major dealers or auction houses, is unlikely to have been stolen. On the other hand, an item for which no provenance is available is questionable, especially where the dealer refuses to disclose how he or she obtained it.

Careful buyers demand express, written representations relating to provenance. Indeed, some experts contend that buyers of art and collectibles should inquire into provenance and should be considered "good faith" buyers only if they do so diligently. This is not the law in any US state. Indeed, in the *Porter* case we referred to earlier, the Art Dealers Association of America (ADAA) filed an *amicus curiae* brief "arguing that the ordinary custom in the art business is not to inquire as to title and that a duty of inquiry would cripple the art business. . . ." Nothing has changed in the nearly forty years since *Porter* was decided, and the ADAA recently filed a similar amicus brief in another New York case. Of course, it makes good sense to inquire into the seller's title before making a major purchase. But if you buy from a reputable dealer, you may rely on the absence of unusual circumstances to protect your title to art or collectibles from claims by prior owners.

SUMMARY

Keep the following in mind to ensure good title is passed with your transaction:

- Good title protects the buyer from any third party claiming a right to the goods you just paid full price for.

- When a third party claims the goods you bought were stolen from them, you will have to surrender the item and your only remedy is to pursue the seller for your money back.
- While the warranty of title is implied in every sale, it has several disadvantages:
  1. It can be disclaimed by the seller in the contract;
  2. It only entitles the buyer to get money damages from the seller (and presumes the seller will have said money); and
  3. It only covers third party claims brought within the first four years that the buyer owns the item.
- If the dealer has authorization to sell the goods on behalf of the owner, claims as to title from that owner may be voidable because the owner bears the risk of finding a trustworthy dealer to which to consign.

5

Buying Art and Collectibles for Investment

It's human nature to hope that the things we collect will increase in value over time. However, in recent years art and collectibles have been bought by investors who are primarily interested in profits, or sold by dealers who tout their value as investments. Investors are often not as knowledgeable about art and collectibles as are collectors, and a profit motive sometimes obscures common sense and good judgment. We won't take a position on whether art and collectibles are good investments—they certainly can be under the right circumstances. This chapter alerts would-be investors to some common areas of trouble when buying art or collectibles for investment and explains some basic rights you may have as an investor. But remember an important distinction between this chapter and chapters 2 and 3. All buyers of art and collectibles are entitled to enforce dealers' express and implied warranties, but those who buy for investment may have certain *additional* rights.

MISREPRESENTATIONS VERSUS LITERAL TRUTH

It is unlawful to sell art and collectibles as investments by inducing investors to overpay for those items with misrepresentations of material fact. "Misrepresentations" are statements of fact that are untrue at the time they are made. As was discussed for express warranties, art and collectibles invite statements of subjective opinions by dealers, and subjective interpretations of those statements by the buyer. *Statements of opinion* that turn out to be untrue are not misrepresentations. Recall the example from chapter 2 of the dealer who says that a painting is "the best" work from Picasso's "blue period." If the work was, in fact, from the blue period, the fact that another art expert—or *most* art experts—do not agree that it is "the best" does not make the dealer's statement a misrepresentation. Likewise, as with express warranties of authenticity, if the statement was true at the time based on available knowledge and scholarship, the fact that it is subsequently proven false does not convert a good faith statement into a misrepresentation.

Notwithstanding the above, investors are often deceived by statements of fact which, though literally true, are misleading without additional information. The sales pitches of fraudulent retailers of art and collectibles are full of such half-truths and misleading statements. The law recognizes this, and consequently, the *omission* of necessary factual information is the equivalent of an outright misrepresentation where the dealer should have known that the result would be statements that are misleading to the average investor.

Here are some examples of truths, untruths, half-truths, and statements of opinion relating to the sale of rare coins:

- "This 1751 coin was salvaged from the sunken treasure ship *Vliegenhart*." Because the *Vliegenhart* sank in 1735, this statement likely is untrue and is a misrepresentation.
- "This 2019 Lincoln Cent is the only one certified MS-63 by PCGS." Again, assuming this is literally true, it is nevertheless misleading in implying rarity, because the coin is extremely common. In fact, a 2019 penny is worth so little in any condition other than near-perfect or perfect (MS-69 or MS-70) that the expense of independent PCGS certification is not justified (which, of course, means there aren't going to be many certified).
- "This 1894-S Barber Dime is the only one certified MS-65 by PCGS." Assuming the statement is literally true, the implication that the coin is quite rare is not misleading because the 1894-S dime is, in fact, one of the rarest US coins.

The dealer's intent regarding the misrepresentation—that is, whether he or she *knowingly lied*—is relevant in certain ways, as will be discussed later in the chapter, but does not affect whether an untrue factual statement is a misrepresentation. Nor does it affect whether the dealer has breached the express or implied warranties discussed in chapters 2 and 3. However, for a misrepresentation to constitute investment fraud, as opposed to a breach of warranty, the dealer must have made the statement in bad faith. In the past, the doctrine of "negligent misrepresentation" might have made dealers liable for statements they honestly believed were true, because they "should have known" or with due diligence "could have known" were false. Today, the rule generally followed by the courts is that a misrepresentation must be made either (1) with knowledge that it is false or (2) with a reasonable likelihood combined with "conscious avoidance" of the truth. This means, for example, that an art dealer who has good reason to think a particular work is a fake cannot rely entirely on the prior owner's representation that it is genuine, if authenticity could be easily confirmed one way or the other.

MATERIALITY AND RELIANCE

Not every false statement of fact in connection with the sale of an item for investment is grounds for legal liability. Even if a misrepresentation is made intentionally, it must be "material"; that is, it must relate to something a reasonable buyer would consider important to his or her decision to buy. In other words, if a dealer accurately describes and prices a painting to you, but lies about where he or she studied art history, that would not be a material misrepresentation, unless the dealer's false statements about their prior education included acquiring special expertise in the particular genre of work being offered.

In addition to materiality, an actionable misrepresentation must actually have been reasonably relied upon by the investor prior to making the purchase. Investors who are disappointed with the performance of particular items cannot search the dealer's marketing materials with a fine-toothed comb looking for any possible falsehood upon which to demand their money back. The reliance requirement also means that statements made *after* the purchase are usually not actionable (a clear exception applies to statements made during a return period, upon which the investor relies in deciding to keep the goods and not return them).

Proof of materiality and reliance sometimes depend on the knowledge and sophistication of the investor. The more knowledgeable a buyer is, the less "reasonable" is his or her reliance on a dealer's representations. This sounds unfair, but the law only punishes dealers whose false statements of material fact *cause* the investor's damages. An investor who knows he or she is being lied to cannot use that fact as "insurance" against poor performance of the goods, keeping them if the market goes up and suing the dealer for misrepresentation if the market drops. Armen once represented a rare coin dealer against a professional investor whose other holdings included gold and cattle futures, resort condominiums throughout the world, and classic Mercedes-Benz sports cars. However, we also have represented investors who bought art and collectibles with little to no knowledge of investments. The law takes into account that less-knowledgeable investors are more easily fooled.

PRICING (AND OVERPRICING) ART AND COLLECTIBLES FOR INVESTMENT

Beyond both materiality and reliance, an investor must also show that the misrepresentations resulted in his or her overpaying for the item. Most investment fraud claims relating to art or collectibles are brought after the investor learns that the item is not worth what he or she paid for it. But that differential could have been caused by a drop in the item's market value since the time of purchase. The investor must prove that the difference is due to the item having been overpriced when he or she bought it.

This principle bears repeating. Even if the investor can prove that he or she relied on the dealer's material misrepresentations about an item, if the dealer charged a fair price for the item there is no investment fraud claim. A breach of warranty claim would still exist, and the buyer might be entitled to return the item for his or her money back. But that claim would have to be made in accordance with the restrictions and statutes of limitations that apply to warranty claims. Without overpricing, an investment fraud claim simply does not exist.

While valuing particular art and collectibles is far beyond the scope of this book, it is common sense that the greater any item is "marked up" over its fair market value, the more the market value of the item must rise for the investor to sell at a profit. Investors must understand that there is a retail markup on every art or collectibles purchase. Dealers are not charities, and they are entitled to make a profit. In addition, in many cases, special premiums for art and collectible items are quite justified. *Overpricing* occurs in two instances: (1) when the markup is so high that the dealer's representations regarding level of investment risk and appreciation potential become misleading or false; (2) where the dealer's representations about pricing itself are false. In either case, the goods must be marketed as investments, not simply as collectible items. As Barry Cutler, former director of the Federal Trade Commission's (FTC's) Bureau of Consumer Protection, used to say, a dealer can sell "collectible" pencils for one thousand dollars apiece. However, Cutler quickly pointed out that if the pencils were sold *as investments*, the FTC would require that all material representations about them were correct.

The basics of art and collectibles pricing are simple. To the wholesale (dealer-to-dealer) price of the item, the dealer adds a markup reflecting his overhead and profit and, occasionally, the commission paid to a broker, financial planner, or consultant involved with the transaction. "Wholesale value" can be loosely defined as the price one knowledgeable dealer would pay another for the item. This price consists of either an item's intrinsic value (in the case of gold and silver bullion items such as Krugerrands which sell at little to no premium), the "bid" price reported on market exchanges (such as the Certified Coin Exchange for numismatic coins) or in dealer trade publications, or a recent auction price indicative of market value. Where an item is fairly illiquid (as are many art or collectible items), wholesale value is measured by what an investor who owned the item would get for it if he had a reasonable time to show it around in the marketplace. Remember that wholesale value is only one determinant of *fair market value*. Dealers are entitled to a fair markup over wholesale value, although what is "fair" depends on a great many things, including services provided by the dealer, inventorying costs, market volatility, and credit terms. A dealer who searches out a particular painting or rare stamp for a customer may be entitled to more than one who takes one of a thousand Krugerrands in his vault and hands it over (although one shouldn't underestimate the costs of maintaining large inventories even of common items).

But regardless of how much the dealer marks up an item for retail sale, investors in art and collectibles nearly always must sell at wholesale prices, unless they are prepared to consign their property and wait a considerable time to be paid. That means that in order to be promoted as low-risk investments, the markups must be such that the investor can profit in a moderate market upswing. As the court put it in *FTC v. Solomon Trading Co., Inc.*,[1] a case involving fraudulent sales of Erte lithographs: "[W]hen an investment has to double or triple in value before any gain can be realized, it is neither a good investment nor a low-risk investment." In that case, the court found that the dealer had marked up the lithographs 100 percent over their wholesale price, and charged clients a 10 percent commission on resale, and that this made the dealer's representations regarding profit potentially deceptive.

Generally speaking, art and collectibles are sold for 10 percent to 100 percent over their wholesale value. Bullion items carry the smallest markups, followed by rare coins and stamps, and proceeding to higher-markup items such as art and antiquities. The costs of maintaining illiquid inventory and the need to find the "right" buyer in order to maximize price discourage dealers from paying high prices to stock even the works of art they themselves previously sold. Likewise, investors should be skeptical of dealers who say they are retailing art or collectibles at "below wholesale." In such cases, industry grading and pricing standards usually have not been met. FTC consumer pamphlets frequently quote the old adage: "If it sounds too good to be true, it probably isn't." Investors should also be skeptical of claims that daily shifts in the collectibles market require prompt action to "lock in" at a low price. Collectibles, other than items such as bullion coins, whose value is pegged to world gold and silver prices, rarely fluctuate much in value from day to day. And feverish claims by salesmen are usually intended also to suggest that selling will be easy when the time comes. It often isn't.

This brings me to the subject of the premiums themselves. Investors need to understand the amount of premium, its justification, and whether the general marketplace also recognizes it. Many years ago, Armen received a Disney products catalogue. In it were numerous

---

1 FTC v. Solomon Trading Co., Inc., No. 91-cv-1184-PHX-SMM (D. Ariz. 1994), 1994 Trade Regulation Reports ¶ 70,627.

"limited edition" products, such as a "Pooh 30th Anniversary Coin," described in the catalogue as follows:

> **EDITION 3,000 LIMIT**
>
> **New Pooh 30th Anniversary Coin**
>
> Proof-quality, one troy-ounce.999 silver. This **Catalog Exclusive** numbered, limited edition medallion commemorating Winnie the Pooh and the Honey Tree is dated 1966–1996 and double-struck with Disney art from Pooh's first film. Pooh (as raincloud) balloons to the honey . . . enjoys a smackeral on reverse. 1½" diameter. Liberty Mint mark. **Edition: 3,000**. Velvet box. **Certificate of Authenticity. $75**

The intrinsic value of a one-ounce silver coin was approximately five dollars on the day Armen received the catalogue (and is less than thirty dollars today). So the buyer of this coin was paying a huge premium at the time, and a pretty substantial one were the coin on the market today (which it is—as you'll soon see). For a collector who doesn't plan to sell, perhaps having the coin (and the velvet box) is worth it. But the catalogue description seems addressed toward someone thinking about the coin as an investment. The number minted and the Certificate of Authenticity are only relevant to someone who is thinking ahead to selling the coin (after all, the catalogue comes from Disney itself, so the item is surely "authentic"!). Given the intrinsic value, the velvet box, the fact that only three thousand were minted, *and* the Certificate of Authenticity, is the coin a good investment at seventy-five dollars? Only if after a reasonable holding period, a willing buyer can be found at more than seventy-five dollars. That doesn't seem to be the case, however, because a specimen of this coin has been languishing for weeks on an online platform with a "buy it now" price of $47.95. The implications of this example will be discussed in the section on "Liquidity" later in the chapter.

Getting the best price may involve comparison shopping, or some bargaining with the dealer. It also requires knowing the total transaction costs involved with a particular item. As in the securities field, some art and collectibles dealers charge less up front, but commit investors to annual "portfolio management fees," which can be quite expensive. With relatively illiquid items such as art and collectibles there rarely is much real "management" going on, anyway. And will the dealer charge a commission on resale? If, as in the *FTC v. Solomon Trading* case, the combination of markups and commissions requires spectacular—and unlikely—upward market movements in order to break even, the item is overpriced as an investment. Ask dealers to explain their pricing structure, and *look for dealers who do so without your asking.*

PAST APPRECIATION STATISTICS

Some art and collectibles are marketed to investors through the use of market price data indicating that the items have appreciated, or can be expected to appreciate, in value. The source and reliability of such data are quite important to its credibility. In addition, dealers should avoid misleading use of past appreciation statistics by explaining any extraordinary events that may skew the figures.

Here's an example. For many years, rare coins were the highest performers in an annual survey conducted by Salomon Brothers, the Wall Street investment bankers. In ten-year and twenty-year studies, rare coins increased in value more than Chinese porcelain, rare stamps, stocks, real estate, and various other categories of investments tracked by Salomon Brothers. Thousands of investors relied on reprints of these studies to invest in rare coins. Unfortunately, Salomon's figures were useless without a thorough knowledge of the methodology used to create them. As it turned out, the coins appraised every year were quite esoteric, and nothing like the types of coins marketed to investors. In addition, price guides such as the Coin Dealer Newsletter, which were used by Salomon, were themselves skewed by steadily more conservative grading interpretations, which resulted in a phenomenon that Scott Travers, a friend of ours and leading writer on numismatic investing, described as follows more than twenty years ago:

> Grading standards are far stricter now than they were in the early days of the Salomon survey. In view of this, the "apples" of bygone years really may be lesser-grade "oranges" by today's more stringent yardstick.

And Salomon also did not remind investors that the apparent steady increases in rare coin prices hid some major market crashes in particular years and that the prices of gold and silver bullion had increased many times during the life of the survey, an increase that was tied to the world metals markets and was highly unlikely to recur. As a result, the FTC targeted the Salomon survey in its Consumer Alert on rare coins:

> Dishonest dealers often mislead buyers by quoting appreciation rates for rare coins from an index formerly compiled each year by Salomon Brothers, a New York investment bank. These quotes show appreciation of 12 percent to 25 percent a year. However, the Salomon index was based on a list of twenty very rare coins, while the coins sold by dishonest dealers are more common coins that are not likely to appreciate at the same rate, if at all. However, almost all dealers, legitimate and dishonest alike, have used the Salomon quotes. . . . Remember, there is no guarantee that any coin will appreciate in value.

In the *Solomon Trading* case discussed above, the art dealer (who was not affiliated in any way with Salomon Brothers) used "performance charts" that supported its salesmen's statements that when Erte prints were released to the public, "the price normally goes up generally anywhere from 23 to 30 percent . . . ten out of ten times."

Another problem in tracking the history of art and collectibles market prices is the extreme thinness of those markets at particular moments. As particular genres are promoted at different times, and cash enters or leaves the markets, prices react, and not always predictably. Therefore, the market trends from prior years are not immediately relevant to present or future price rises. And many collectibles have no organized "secondary market" at all, meaning that increased retail prices do not translate to increased wholesale or resale prices. Armen and Laura often are asked to review marketing materials for sellers of art and collectibles, and a frequent complaint of ours is that the use of isolated transactions on eBay or other platforms doesn't reflect "market value" any more than would any other small, unscientific group of data.

We are very skeptical of any art and collectible dealer who uses rosy past appreciation statistics as the core of its marketing pitch. These markets are simply too unpredictable, and the items themselves too illiquid, to rely on the past performance. Also, as an investor you must ask whether the items tracked by these figures are exactly the types of items you are being offered. It is not enough to sell a living artist's works at a high premium because other artists' works have appreciated in value upon their deaths. Look for discussions of past appreciation that are specific, qualified, and recognize the ups and downs of every investor marketplace, including art and collectibles. A former client of ours (now, sadly out of business) used to print the following on the back of its customer invoices:

> Various graphs and charts are available as to the performance of coins. The data and basis of those reports must be carefully studied to determine whether the document reflects the performance of the type of coins purchased by the potential investor.
>
> Investment in coins is generally considered a long-term investment, that is, the purchaser must typically hold the coins for several years to have a return of his investment. There is no guarantee that the simple holding of a coin for any period will result in appreciation, as interest in particular series, type, metal, mintage or date may change over the period.

LIQUIDITY

Investors in art and collectibles are often confused when it comes to liquidity. Depending again on the type of item, art and collectible items can be extremely *illiquid.* The importance of that fact to a prospective investor in such items cannot be underestimated, and many court cases have arisen over misrepresentations in this area. We recommend you ask five questions when it comes to liquidity of investment art and collectibles: (1) If I am quoted a market value for an item, is there a willing buyer at that price? (2) Who is that buyer and can I reach him or her? (3) Is that buyer financially able to buy the item at the price? (4) What are the transaction costs involved in selling to that buyer? (5) What is the turn-around time? These questions, in turn, raise a host of other questions, and getting answers is crucial to proper investor education.

Put very simply, no market price valuation is meaningful to an investor unless there is a willing buyer at that price. It is in the very nature of most art and collectible items that they are difficult to sell. Only precious metals have an "exchange" comparable to that which exists for common stocks. Rare coins have an active marketplace consisting of dealers connected by computer networks and meeting face to face at shows throughout the country. But much of the lure of art and collectibles comes from their uniqueness or rarity—that is, the fact that what we're buying isn't so common that it is sold by the thousands every day.

Investors in such items pay a big price for that. Even relatively common items are sometimes illiquid when dealers lack cash and/or do not need inventory. A perfect example is post-1940 US postage stamps. Armen has a nice collection of three-, four-, five-, and six-cent commemorative and regular issue stamps from the period 1940–1975 in full mint sheets. But while the catalogue value of, say, a mint 1953 three-cent General Patton stamp (Scott #1026) may be eight or nine cents, he can't sell his fifty-stamp full sheet for fifty times nine cents—that is, $4.50. In fact, he'd be very happy to sell it at $1.50, the *face value* of the stamps. There aren't enough buyers to absorb the plentiful supply of these stamps, making the catalogue values relatively useless.

A recent article in a popular stamp trade publication discussed how many people who inherit collections from their relatives derive totally unrealistic estimates of the value of these inheritances by looking at catalogues. This is far less true with rare coins which, no matter how common, nevertheless have published buy prices from reputable dealers that reflect the strength of the rare coin market. But it can be very much the case with art. Here's another personal example. Armen has a lovely painting by a popular artist, and every New York gallery he's called tells him how great the painting is, and that it is worth at least 50 percent more than he paid twenty years ago. But none wants to handle it for Armen. So, what is Armen's painting actually worth? Nothing, until there is a willing buyer.

Investors must be particularly concerned with collectibles items that have little to no intrinsic value but carry large premiums because of their perceived rarity. Rarity is double-edged. All else being equal, true rarities will have a broader resale market than more common examples of similar items. The 1893-S Morgan Dollar is considerably more marketable than the 1881-S, because far fewer exist. Unlike Armen's stamps and painting, a true rarity has value to enough people that willing buyers can be found easily. But what will these willing buyers pay? The true rarity carries a different liquidity problem for the investor. It must sell at a premium, because the investor paid a premium to purchase it. Therefore, it cannot just be sold to any willing buyer. It must be offered to the right buyer who will pay its full value. This takes time, and adds a certain illiquidity to the item. An extreme example would be the eleven Kennedy half dollars purchased at the Jackie Onassis auction for $8,645 (including the 15 percent buyer's fee). These coins had a retail value of approximately ten dollars, and Sotheby's estimated them at two hundred to three hundred dollars. Are these coins liquid at $8,645? We would say absolutely not. The provenance of these coins, combined with their depiction of President Kennedy, caused the buyer to pay a huge premium. Of course, at the auction there was at least one underbidder at the next lower bidding increment, and probably many others who bid more than ten dollars. Somehow Sotheby's found these people, but how would the present owner of these coins do so? Even auctioning the coins again at Sotheby's would not work. The atmosphere of the Onassis auction was one of near-hysteria, and it will not be duplicated in any resale of her property. It is inconceivable to us that Onassis's Kennedy halves would sell for more than eight thousand dollars again.

Recall the seventy-five-dollar Winnie the Pooh "coin" discussed earlier in this chapter. To be a good investment, the medallion must be marketable within a reasonable period of time at a higher price. So before buying this medallion from Disney, an investor might ask, who will ever pay me more than seventy-five dollars for this? Probably not a coin dealer, because the item isn't a coin, and a coin dealer is unlikely to accept that so large a premium should attach to a contemporary piece. The dealer would pay intrinsic (silver) value, maybe even a little less to cover the cost of handling. Disney? Disney does not make a two-way market in its collectibles. An antique or collectibles dealer? The truth is that there's no "secondary market" in this type of item, and if Disney is fortunate enough to sell all three thousand Pooh "coins" from its catalogue, the buyers will never know if they can get more than the intrinsic value on resale.

Assuming this is an item for which a resale market exists and can be identified, and there is some general agreement about market value. Is the item liquid at the market price? Certainly, if the buyer has ready cash for immediate purchase and there are no transaction costs. Here's an example. Armen called Christie's some time ago about selling some old Leica camera equipment. Christie's telephoned him back with an estimate of five hundred to seven hundred pounds for the material, which they later confirmed in writing. But can Armen sell his camera equipment at that price now? Possibly, but Christie's was not offering to buy it. Christie's was simply offering to accept the equipment for consignment to one of its photography sales to take place in London later in the year. No guarantees were made, and the equipment could sell for less, without even taking into account the commissions Christie's would take on the sale, and Armen's costs in getting the items to London. As will be discussed later, finding a dealer to pay cash for an art or collectible item is difficult, even where the item has a recognized value. For our purposes in this chapter, remember that liquidity involves a realistic assessment of how long an investor must wait to find someone willing to pay market value when it is time to sell.

The final point about liquidity relates to the mechanics of sale: transaction costs and turn-around time. Even relatively liquid items such as shares of IBM common stock cannot be sold instantaneously with no transaction costs, unless one has a seat on the New York Stock Exchange. But stock is considerably more liquid than art or collectibles. If someone sells IBM shares today, the broker will confirm the trade almost instantaneously, and the investor will have access to the proceeds—minus a very small commission—within a day or two, sometimes less. When selling investment art or collectibles, commissions and turn-around times can be astonishing, depending on how and through whom you sell.

Catalogues may not reflect the actual market price of art and collectibles. But lack of liquidity also makes dealer appraisals and "portfolio updates" suspect, unless the dealer is actually offering to buy at the prices given. Auction estimates must likewise be read with some skepticism when the proposed auction is months away. Moreover, investors must understand that there are transaction costs involved with selling their art and collectibles, such as dealer or auctioneer commissions. Liquidity at a certain price is only relevant if that price is *net* of these transaction costs.

A candid discussion of liquidity issues for rare coins, which is even more true for other forms of collectibles, can be found in Heritage Auctions' excellent disclosures in its Terms and Conditions of Auction:

> The degree of liquidity for certified coins and collectibles will vary according to general market conditions and the particular lot involved. For some lots there may be no active market at all at certain periods of time.

BUYBACKS AND PORTFOLIO "UPDATES"

Some dealers advertise buyback policies—that is, commitments to repurchase any item they sell on certain terms and conditions. These policies can demonstrate the dealer's faith in its goods, and they can give investors confidence that a two-way market exists in the items they are purchasing. However, buyback policies require some skepticism. When the buyback policy is joined by a policy of providing periodic portfolio updates, you must ask yourself (and the dealer) certain questions.

First, what do the updates and buyback prices mean? Dealers like to use "replacement value" in their updates. That is, the update tells the investor what he or she would have to pay to buy the item at retail that particular day. *Replacement value is not what the dealer would pay you for your item.* The difference between the dealer's "ask" and "bid" depends on a lot of things, and is roughly the same as the difference between wholesale and retail described above. It can be substantial. For most art or collectible items, a 20 percent increase in replacement value still means you would suffer a loss if you sold. Without some explanation, replacement value is not an accurate measure of an item's appreciation.

Second, does the dealer have the reserves necessary to finance its buybacks? A buyback commitment is only as strong as the person giving it. Even where the dealer only offers to pay wholesale value, the costs of inventorying an indefinite—and potentially unlimited—amount of material are immense. As the court noted in *FTC v. Security Rare Coin & Bullion Corp.*:[2]

> In order to allay concerns about investing in rare coins, defendants represented to consumers that they maintained a buy-back policy, whereby Security would buy back coins from its customers at a discount off the company's prevailing sales prices.
>
> . . .
>
> defendants did not maintain a reserve of funds to satisfy buy-back requests. If only ten percent of defendants' customers had sought to take advantage of the buy-back, defendants would have had insufficient funds to satisfy their requests.

Of course, it's known that banks could not satisfy more than a small fraction of their depositors closing their accounts all at once. However, a dealer in investment art and collectibles must be able to back up a buy-back guarantee. Investments, by definition, will peak at certain times, and when selling any genre of art or collectible, the entire genre is likely to peak together. Look for firms that offer to provide audited financial

---

[2] FTC v. Security Rare Coin & Bullion Corp., 931 F.2d 1312 (8th Cir. 1991).

information about themselves before you buy, and ask them to explain how they manage buying back the items they sell.

Third, where buybacks are promised at *more* than the wholesale value, the red flags should be up. Some honest retailers will offer their clients more for art and collectible items than will other dealers because they are more familiar with the items being offered. Offers from a dealer who has actually handled an item will generally be higher than those from dealers who are basing their offers on photographs or telephone descriptions. However, there is always a built-in incentive for retail investment firms to offer clients more than fair market value for their portfolios, to make clients believe that they have profited and to encourage more purchases. But that begins to look like a Ponzi scheme, where yesterday's investors are paid back with today's investors' capital. A rare coin dealer in Southern California provided customers with buyback prices every month and offered an additional 18 percent premium over those prices if the customer waited thirty days for payment. Such a premium is totally unjustified and represented a blatant effort to convince customers that the market was rising so fast that they should not sell at all.

Fourth, when investors want to cash in, dealers often try to persuade them to shift their "paper" profits into additional purchases. Additional trades result in more profit to the dealer, and no real benefit to the investor (and maybe some tax liability—we'll see in chapter 18 that there are no more "tax-free" exchanges for art and collectible items). Art and collectibles salesmen can "churn" accounts just like sellers of stocks and bonds.

DEALERS AS FIDUCIARIES

Fiduciaries are professionals who owe a special duty of care to their clients, such that they are absolutely liable for any errors or omissions, whether intentional or not. Generally, with investors a fiduciary relationship arises only where the law requires one (such as in the case of trustees), or where the client reasonably believes that the professional is acting solely in the client's interest and not his or her own.

Generally speaking, art and collectibles dealers are not fiduciaries of their customers, and there is abundant case law to the effect that just because those dealers may know more about the goods they sell than their customers doesn't give them any special obligation to ensure that customers earn a profit on their purchases. See *Mechigian v. Art Capital Corp.*[3] Dealers make retail sales of goods to customers to earn a profit for themselves, and do not act primarily for the benefit of their customers. More importantly, customers know this to be true, and do not expect dealers to put their own interests below those of their customers. However, it's also the case that a retail art and collectibles dealer has far more influence over an investor's decision making and ultimate success than does a stockbroker or other investment advisor. Stocks are priced by an independent, regulated marketplace and investors have many independently prepared reports and other documents available to them prior to investing. Those who invest in art and collectibles, however, often find that the dealer both selects and prices the investment vehicle and is solely responsible for disclosing the risks. Though not a fiduciary, the dealer who markets art or collectibles as investments has more responsibility than most other sellers of investments. In some cases, this could rise to the level of a fiduciary relationship. In two notable cases, where dealers sold major works of art on behalf of collector clients for more money than they disclosed to the clients—keeping secret profits for themselves—the courts found that a line had been crossed and that the dealers had to disgorge those profits to the clients.

ARE ART OR COLLECTIBLE ITEMS SECURITIES?

Because so many people invest in art and collectibles as part of an overall personal portfolio including stocks, bonds, and other securities, the question has arisen whether art and collectibles dealers have the same responsibilities as sellers of securities. This question has appeared in several court cases, with mixed results.

The leading definition of "security" comes from the US Supreme Court's decision in *SEC v. W.J. Howey Co.*[4] In *Howey,* the Court held that a transaction constitutes a sale of securities if it "involves an investment of money in a common enterprise with profits to come solely from the

---

[3] Mechigian v. Art Capital Corp., 612 F. Supp. 1421 (S.D.N.Y. 1985).

[4] SEC v. W.J. Howey Co., 328 U.S. 293 (1946).

efforts of others."[5] Lower federal courts interpreted *Howey* as requiring that the success or failure of the investment depend on the efforts of others besides the investors.[6] Since *Howey*, a federal appeals court in California has stated that where investors buy collectibles from a retailer, their profits come entirely from fluctuations in the collectibles markets that are out of the dealer's control.[7] In *SEC v. Brigadoon Scotch Distributors, Ltd.*,[8] however, a New York federal district judge found that First Coin Rarities, which sold rare coins, was selling securities:

> [I]t is significant that FCR's advertising brochure . . . consistently described the collection of rare coins as an "investment". Comparisons of gains in the stock market with returns from coins, analysis of coin appreciation and similar investment information run in a constant and main stream throughout FCR's sales pitch. The placement of advertisements in airline magazines and medical journals rather than in numismatic periodicals bolsters the view that the thrust of FCR's efforts are directed at an investing, rather than a coin-collecting, public.[9]

The court emphasized the fact that half of FCR's sales were of coins selected for customers by FCR itself:

> This fact alone persuades us that the third aspect of the Howey test, that is, the dependence of the investor on the expertise of the seller to produce the expected profit, is present here. Coins do not appreciate at the same rate and accordingly their selection is the most crucial factor in determining how much profit an investor in coins will make . . . And the presence of the package of investment advice and information referred to above of course only supports our finding.[10]

---

[5] *Id.* at 301.

[6] SEC v. Glenn W. Turner Enterprises, Inc., 474 F.2d 476, 482 (9th Cir.), *cert. denied*, 414 U.S. 821 (1973).

[7] SEC v. Belmont Reid & Co., Inc., 794 F.2d 1388 (9th Cir. 1986) (gold bullion coins).

[8] SEC v. Brigadoon Scotch Distributors, Ltd., 388 F. Supp. 1288 (S.D.N.Y. 1975).

[9] *Id.* at 1291.

[10] *Id.* at 1293.

Under the *Brigadoon* approach, nearly all art or collectibles dealers who sell primarily to investors will be deemed to be selling securities. Other federal district courts have rejected *Brigadoon* and found that rare coins are not securities. More than twenty years ago Armen litigated the case of *Llewellyn v. North American Trading*, which not only dismissed breach of warranty and fraud claims by an investor against a rare coin dealer, but also found that *Brigadoon* no longer was controlling precedent, and that the appropriate standard was whether the customer's interests were intertwined with the dealer's such that "his or her fortunes would rise with the promoter's fortunes, but also that their fortunes would fall together." Because art and collectibles dealers retain their profits from a transaction even if the customer loses money reselling the goods, a typical retail sale of art and collectibles would not be a security.

The Securities and Exchange Commission, when asked, has chosen a middle path by refusing to issue "no-action" letters—statements that certain types of transactions are not sales of securities—to at least three rare coin and collectibles dealers, while never actually prosecuting such dealers for failing to register. New York State, however, once prosecuted a collectibles dealer for failing to register as a broker-dealer under New York State's securities law, the Martin Act, before selling shares in rare coin, art, and real estate portfolios. And recent trends toward offering high-priced art and collectible items for fractional ownership or through purpose-built corporate structures seem clearly to have crossed the line into investment securities. We aren't against making multi-million-dollar items—and the thrill of owning them—available to collectors and investors of more modest means. Far from it. But federal and state securities regulators require considerably more from sellers of securities than they do of typical retail sellers, and investors have more and different remedies available to them if their investments fail. It's important to know where each transaction fits in this regulatory framework.

The ramifications of art and collectibles being the legal equivalent of securities is beyond the scope of this book, and many of the key concepts of securities fraud litigation—misrepresentations, reliance, causation—have already been discussed earlier in this chapter. We don't think that the legal authorities so far give any clear picture on this point, and it simply remains one possible argument for investors to raise, and for promoters to consider before making sales.

SUMMARY

If you are ready to buy art or collectibles as an investment, keep the following in mind:

- What sounds too good true to be true probably isn't.
- Understand the concept of liquidity and do not buy illiquid items unless you don't expect to ever have to sell quickly.
- Understand the retail markups by learning exactly what you would get if you sold the item the day after purchase.
- Carefully review all representations relating to grade, condition, and rarity, and make sure they are based on industrywide standards, or are correlated to industrywide standards.
- Look for balanced presentations regarding past performance statistics, understanding that in every market there are ups and downs.
- Find out the dealer's refund and repurchase policy and, remembering that these policies are only as strong as the dealer itself, ask for financial information about the dealer.
- Don't do business with dealers who are reluctant to give you the information you need to make a purchase.

6

Selling Art or Collectibles through Dealers

Many collectors and investors choose to sell art or collectibles through a dealer rather than an auction house. There are various reasons for this, including prior relationship with the dealer, the prospect of prompt sale and settlement, and a dealer's special ability to find buyers of rare or unusual pieces. In choosing a dealer through whom to sell, consider such factors as years in business, reputation, special expertise with the type of item, and professional affiliations. If the item is very valuable, by all means interview the dealer personally and ask questions. And keep in mind the principles discussed below.

THE BUYER AS RESELLER: WARRANTIES

If a sale is outright, a simple contract or bill of sale is sufficient to document the sale. As a nondealer, you will not be bound to many of the legal rules and regulations discussed in chapters 2 and 3 for retail sales by dealers. For example, you will not make implied warranties of merchantability, because under the Uniform Commercial Code (UCC) such warranties are only implied into sales by "merchants in the particular goods." This fact also makes disclaimer of warranties easier for collector-sellers than it is for dealers. In addition, nondealers ordinarily are not required to collect or pay sales or use taxes in connection with their sales of art or collectibles, because they are considered "occasional sellers" for tax purposes. Finally, a dealer will be held to have the same or superior knowledge of the field compared to a nondealer, such that typically the dealer cannot claim to have been deceived by misleading statements from the seller regarding an item.

However, the basic rules of contract law that govern all sales of goods will still apply. This was made clear in the case of *Feigen & Co. v. Weil,*[1] where Richard Feigen, a prominent New York art dealer, purchased a drawing from an art collector for $100,000, and resold it to a client for $165,000, believing it to be by Matisse. When the client showed the drawing to another gallery, the gallery checked with the Matisse estate and discovered that the drawing was a forgery. Feigen immediately refunded the client's $165,000, but had to sue the collector to recover his $100,000. The collector argued that Feigen, as a dealer, could have checked with the Matisse estate himself before buying the drawing, and therefore Feigen should bear the risk of a "mutual mistake" regarding authenticity. The court disagreed and ruled in Feigen's favor, stating that a mutual mistake in the sale of art is, indeed, just that, regardless of whether the injured buyer happens to be the dealer rather than the collector. Note that this decision isn't entirely consistent with the ACA decision discussed in chapter 2, where the federal court might well have asked why Feigen hadn't himself checked with the Matisse estate before buying the painting in the first place.[2]

CONSIGNMENTS TO DEALERS: TERMS AND CONDITIONS

However, usually dealers do not buy art or collectible items outright. Rather, they agree to take them on consignment. Consignment is the legal term for transferring to another person the right to sell one's property. In the case of art or collectibles dealers, a consignment agreement provides that the dealer will be paid a commission for finding a buyer and concluding a sale of the property. The terms and conditions of

[1] Feigen & Co. v. Weil, 191 A.D.2d 278 (N.Y. App. Div. 1993).

[2] ACA Galleries v. Kinney, 928 F.Supp.2d 699 (S.D.N.Y. 2013), aff'd, 552 Fed. Appx. 24 (2d Cir. 2014).

consignment agreements are quite important, and as with the contract of sale itself, they should be negotiated carefully and put in writing.

The first term is whether the consignment is what attorneys call an "exclusive right to sell." In other words, is the dealer the only person who may sell the item during the period of the consignment, or do you reserve rights to sell the item yourself or through another dealer? Many dealers will not take consignments without exclusive rights, because they fear making extensive efforts to sell only to learn that another dealer (or the owner) sold the item and no commission is due them.

The next term is the length of the consignment. Sellers want results, and it is fair to limit the length of time that a particular dealer has to survey its clients and promote the item. On the other hand, works of art or rare collectibles often do not find their optimum buyer quickly, and they will not achieve their best prices if the seller appears too anxious. Take the dealer's advice and be clear on your own financial needs. If the desired price is not obtained within the agreed time, the consignment is terminated. In some consignments, the item is immediately returned to the owner. In others, the dealer is required to purchase the item at a pre-agreed price, generally less than the price at which the dealer advertised the item to the public. The latter works better for collectors who do not want the property back and are willing to discount a little to have a sale.

Of course, the commission rate is also a crucial term. Commissions vary with the customs and mechanics of different markets. The commission on sales of fine art paintings may be considerably higher than that of more liquid items such as rare coins. In some cases, the collector or investor will set a desired price, and will award the dealer a higher commission as an incentive if he or she is able to sell the item for a higher price. Conversely, if the dealer receives an offer lower than the desired price, the collector/investor might agree to it on condition that the dealer reduce his or her commission.

THE ENTRUSTER RULE: PROTECTING YOURSELF

One crucial aspect of consigning property to a dealer is protection against the "entruster" rule and claims by the dealer's other creditors. As discussed in chapter 4 in the context of buying art or collectibles, the entruster rule allows dealers to pass good title to consigned goods, regardless of whether the dealer has complied with the terms of a consignment agreement with the owner. For example, a collector may consign paintings to a dealer based on the dealer's agreement to pay the collector 50 percent of the sale price within thirty days of any sale. If the dealer sells a painting and does not pay, the collector can no longer demand return of the painting, has no rights whatsoever against the buyer of the painting, and is left only with a damages claim against the dealer.

The entruster rule extends even to cases where the property was not consigned for sale but entrusted to a dealer for another purpose. It is common in the art and collectibles industry for dealers to perform other services. For example, an art dealer may take possession to appraise a painting; an antique furniture dealer may also take possession of furniture that the owner wants restored, not sold; and coin and sports card dealers often take possession of items in order to submit them to an authentication and grading service. In all such circumstances, the entruster rule provides that if the dealer sells the item despite the fact that the item was not consigned to be sold, the owner cannot demand return of the item from the buyer, only money damages against the dealer. This is because the person with possession of the item is also in the business of selling that item and therefore the buyer is entitled to presume that the dealer is authorized to complete the sale.

Note that the entruster rule only applies if the person selling the item is a dealer of the type of goods entrusted and the owner of the item knows the seller is a dealer. In the case of *Abbott Laboratories v. Feinberg*,[3] Abbott maintained an art collection of approximately two hundred works, many of which were sent to CAA, an art restoration company, in the 1980s. Decades later, Abbott learned that many of the works that had been "restored" by CAA, including *Maine Flowers* by Marsden Hartley, had in fact been stolen and replaced with forgeries. When Abbott located *Maine Flowers* in the possession of the Feinberg family, Abbott brought an action to recover the painting. Feinberg asserted the entruster rule as a defense. However, the court found that there was no evidence (of which Feinberg bore the burden of proving) that Abbott knew CAA sold art in addition to restoring it. Therefore, the

---

[3] Abbott Laboratories v. Feinberg, No. 18-8468 (S.D.N.Y. Dec. 9, 2020).

court declined to apply the entruster rule and ultimately found Abbott to have superior title to *Maine Flowers.*

In addition to the risk of a dealer passing title to consigned goods under the entruster rule, there is also the risk that consigned goods will be seized to satisfy claims by the dealer's secured creditors, which can include everyone from the Internal Revenue Service to another consignor. Dealers who rely on bank financing generally give the lender a security interest in their office fixtures, accounts receivable, and inventory. Because a dealer's inventory includes consigned goods, should the dealer default on his loan payments, the bank might well be able to seize property on consignment to sell in order to satisfy the debt.

An interesting case involved a Minneapolis rare coin dealer, which was placed into receivership after a lawsuit by the Federal Trade Commission (FTC). The federal district court judge appointed Armen as the receiver, and it was his job to investigate claims concerning hundreds of rare coins the company held as inventory. It turned out that many of the company's customers were investors, and the company offered them commission-free sales of their coins. Unfortunately, the company rarely paid promptly after the sales. Armen's investigations revealed that a substantial number of coins consigned by customers had been sold and the customers were not even notified, much less paid. Others were not sold, but were held as inventory for sale, and the company borrowed against them and actually shipped them to the bank as collateral until the loans were paid off. Even after the bank was paid and released the coins, as court-appointed receiver Armen's rights to the consigned coins were superior to those of the customers who had originally consigned the coins, and this carried through when a bankruptcy trustee took over for Armen. The customers had nothing other than a creditor's claim for return of their purchase price. Instead of getting their coins back, they got pennies on the dollar.

Art and collectibles consignors often ask how they can protect their property in such situations. This is a complicated question, but remembering some simple rules will help avoid trouble. And as with most things, the best defenses are implemented at the time of the original consignment rather than later when the property is at risk.

First, to give notice of the consignment to the dealer's other (potential) creditors, you may want to file a UCC-1 financing statement. This is a simple form identifying the "debtor" (the dealer receiving the consignment), the "secured party" (the collector who owns the item being consigned) and the "collateral" (the property being sold). Many items consigned together can be included in the same UCC-1 form, and fortunately over the past few years the laws concerning UCC-1s have changed in two ways favoring consignors: (1) the debtor's (dealer's) signature is no longer required; (2) the form need be filed only with the appropriate agency in the state where the dealer's principal place of business is located. Collectors consigning any sizable value of art or collectibles may wish to file a UCC-1 financing statement, or have an attorney do it for them.

Second, spend the time and money to prepare a written consignment agreement rather than scribble something on a "receipt" or other generic document. That way, you'll say what you need to say, and everyone (including a court or government attorney) can see that the consignment is legally effective. Most "memo" agreements I've seen dealers using simply wouldn't stand up in court to protect the consignor. State laws resolve any doubts in favor of the consignee's creditors (i.e., against the consignor) when the consignee is a dealer. The law disregards such phrases as "on consignment" or "on memorandum," or the commonly used "title does not pass until payment in full" when considering claims of prior creditors or the government.

Third, beware of the dealer commingling your property with his or her other inventory. For unique works of art this isn't a concern. But when your collection of one hundred Morgan silver dollars ends up in inventory along with someone else's, maintaining title and/or security in your material becomes more complicated. The law provides only an imperfect solution here, but you can still protect yourself in most cases. If there are serial numbers or other identifying marks affixed or accompanying the item, note them in the consignment agreement and any UCC-1s.

Fourth, get good information about the dealer. A UCC search will give you a printout of all the dealer's prior secured creditors—copies of all UCC-1s and any related filings—at a minimal cost, and we recommend this before any major consignment. Staying alert to the dealer's financial difficulties is also crucial. Although collectors should make security arrangements before turning over their property, "better late than never" applies too.

SUMMARY

Consider the following when selling through a dealer:

- Consignment agreements should be in writing and include:
  - Whether the dealer has the exclusive right to sell the item during the period of time.
  - The length of time the dealer has to sell the items consigned.
  - The minimum agreed price the dealer may sell the item for.
  - The commission rate and whether costs (such as authenticating an item) will be covered by the dealer or consignor.
- Filing a UCC-1 financing statement will protect the consignor against the dealer selling the item in violation of the consignment agreement.

7

Miscellaneous Aspects of Buying Art or Collectibles

This chapter discusses certain aspects of buying art and collectibles that are important but are not treated with the same detail as the others. For most buyers and sellers, these should not be a problem, but a buyer or seller should be aware that the issues may arise under certain circumstances.

MORAL RIGHTS

In addition to restrictions on reproduction rights based on copyright law, discussed in chapter 11, the owner of a work of art might be limited in his or her use of that work by an artist's "moral rights." Moral rights, also known by the French term *droit moral*, include, among other things, artists' rights to regulate how their works are displayed and to protect their works from destruction or mutilation even after ownership of the work itself and/or its copyright are transferred to third parties.

Moral rights are a European invention and are embodied in international treaties as well as various foreign statutes. In the United States, a moral rights movement resulted in legislation being enacted in several states during the 1980s. These state enactments attempted to balance artists' rights with the property rights held by owners of artwork or of structures in which artwork has been incorporated permanently (such as in the case of murals, mosaics, and certain types of sculptures).

In 1991, the federal Visual Artists' Rights Act (VARA)[1] established a nationwide moral rights regime, in the process preempting portions of the earlier state enactments. In the case of *Carter v. Helmsley-Spear* in 1994,[2] a federal court in New York applied VARA for the first time, enjoining the owner of a commercial office building from removing an unusual sculpture commissioned by a former tenant who had defaulted on its lease and left the building. Other cases have involved a sculpture split in half when its owner decided it took up too much space, a painting displayed next to a museum's fire exit, and a television comedy show that was edited against the wishes and permission of the writer/performer.

Our notions of private property do not easily accept moral rights. Why shouldn't the owner of a sculpture be able to cut it in two if he or she wants to? Of course, moral rights generally apply only to works that are publicly displayed, so presumably sculptures kept in the back yard have less protection than those in the front yard. This, too, seems arbitrary. Moreover, moral rights are personal to the artist, can never be transferred, and do not follow the copyright. This means that even the owner of a work who also owns the copyright cannot do what he or she pleases without potential liability to the artist. The justification for moral rights is the artist's need to protect his or her reputation by making sure works are displayed the way the artist intended them to be. Art collectors must respect this, and the laws are there to provide penalties for art owners who do not. Anyone doubting this should look at the case of *Castillo v. G&M Realty,*[3] where the Second Circuit Court of Appeals affirmed a $6.75 million award against a building owner who whitewashed various graffiti works on the side of a building he owned.

---

[1] 17 U.S.C. §§ 101 *et seq.*

[2] Carter v. Helmsley-Spear, 861 F. Supp. 303 (S.D.N.Y. 1994).

[3] Castillo v. G&M Realty, L.P., 950 F.3d 155 (2d Cir. 2020), *cert. denied,* 141 S.Ct. 363 (2020).

RESALE RIGHTS

European artists receive royalties for subsequent sales of their art—that is, for sales following the initial sale made directly by the artist himself or herself. In countries such as France and Germany, such resale royalties—often referred to by their French name, *droit de suite*—compensate the artist for appreciating values of art over time. It is believed that artists spending much of their careers in obscurity are not properly paid for earlier works that later trade at huge multiples of their original prices. Currently, within the European Union (EU) the resale royalty right derives from Directive 2001/84/EC, and is limited to "original works of art," defined by Article 2 of the Directive as follows:

1. For the purpose of this Directive, "original work of art" means works of graphic or plastic art such as pictures, collages, paintings, drawings, engravings, prints, lithographs, sculptures, tapestries, ceramics, glassware and photographs, provided they are made by the artist himself or are copies considered to be original works of art.
2. Copies of works of art covered by this Directive, which have been made in limited numbers by the artist himself or under his authority, shall be considered to be original works of art for purposes of this Directive. Such copies will normally have been numbered, signed or otherwise duly authorized by the artist.

So even in the EU the obligation to pay resale royalties only applies when dealing with original works of art. We recently advised a group of vintage poster dealers that in most cases, the estates of twentieth-century commercial poster artists would not be entitled to resale royalties because such posters would not meet Directive 2001/84/EC's definition of "original works of art."

The United States never adopted *droit de suite* into law. In fact, while such rights were recognized by the Berne Convention, the international treaty upon which most countries' copyright laws are based—including US copyright law—they were considered so controversial that signatories to the Convention were permitted to opt out of it, which the United States, United Kingdom, and many other countries did.

California adopted a resale royalty law in the mid-1970s (California Civil Code § 986), and remains the only state in which artists—theoretically, at least—were ever entitled to a share (5 percent) of the proceeds of all sales of their works for their lifetime plus twenty years, whether the sale was by a gallery or a private collector. The rights are limited in several ways, however. First, they apply only to the sale of "fine art" which is defined as original paintings, sculptures, and drawings. Second, resale rights applied only where the seller lived in California or the sale itself took place there. Third, sales for less than one thousand dollars, sales at a loss, and sales by a dealer who bought the item directly from the artist were exempt.

An additional complication was the Ninth Circuit Court of Appeals' 2015 decision in *Sam Francis Foundation v. Christie's, Inc. et al.*,[4] which declared § 986 unconstitutional under the Commerce Clause to the extent it applied to sales occurring completely outside California, such as where a California resident consigns a work of art for sale at an auction held in New York. Upon remand, the federal district judge proceeded to invalidate the entire law as being preempted by the Copyright Act, a decision that was affirmed by the Court of Appeals.

SUMMARY

Additional considerations when buying and selling art include:

- Art bought or displayed outside of the United States may carry moral rights that prohibit the buyer from destroying it and ensure the art is displayed as the artist intended.
- Publicly displayed art—including graffiti and television—carries certain moral rights preventing destruction or concealment in the United States.
- If buying or selling art outside of the United States, such as France, there may be a resale royalty requiring a percentage of the sale to be remitted to the artist.

[4] Sam Francis Foundation v. Christie's, Inc. et al., 784 F.3d 1320 (9th Cir. 2015).

PART 2

Buying and Selling Art and Collectibles at Auction

Many people think that only the most expensive art and collectibles are sold at public auction. This is untrue, and public auction is a very popular method for buying and selling all types of art and collectibles. However, it is considerably different in many ways from the retail transactions discussed in the prior chapters, so review chapters 8 and 9 carefully before you decide to buy or sell at auction.

8

Consigning to Auction

Auctioneers bring buyers and sellers together. Beyond that simple statement lies a multibillion-dollar industry. Collectors who wish to sell all or part of their collections know that typically they will achieve the highest price only by exposing the items being sold to the maximum number of other collectors. Where the items are exotic or of only narrow collecting interest, this exposure is even more important, and sellers want what few collectors there are in a particular area to know that the property is for sale. Auctioneers serve the function of advertising the prospective sale of art and collectible property and managing the business aspects of that sale. A professional auction house acts as warehouse, appraiser, insurer, photographer, researcher, bank, salesperson, and credit manager for its consignor, in ways that will be discussed below. For the buyers, the auctioneer is authenticator, appraiser, and delivery service. And even these lists don't do justice to the auctioneer's pivotal role in the art and collectibles industry. The many benefits of public auction explain the highly popular use of that method of sale in the largest art and collectibles transactions.

THE CONSIGNMENT AGREEMENT

Auctions are, in essence, sales of many people's property together. The property is consigned to the auction house for sale, usually pursuant to a written consignment agreement. Although the wording of these agreements varies somewhat among auction houses, certain subjects are nearly always covered, and must be considered in working out the business terms of the consignment.

Exclusive Right to Sell

Auction houses require that consignors give them the exclusive right to sell the items being consigned. This means that consignors cannot withdraw their items from sale except as provided by the consignment agreement. Ordinarily, there is no right to withdraw at all, and consignors may reclaim their own consigned property only if the property fails to meet a reserve bid, or if the consignor buys his or her own property at the sale. The auction house will not undertake the effort of cataloguing and promoting the goods if the consignor has the right to withdraw them or sell them elsewhere. Keeping in mind that auctions usually take place months after the agreement is signed, a consignor choosing between selling directly to a dealer or at public auction takes a gamble that by the time of the auction circumstances will not have changed to his or her detriment. The art and collectibles market is very volatile, and today's favorable trends could become extremely unfavorable while your property awaits auction. Personal circumstances can also change to the point where a quicker sale would be advantageous. Despite the contract provisions, auction house staff are human beings and are sensitive to their consignor's needs and desires. In compelling situations, they will agree to allow withdrawal of items even after they have done most of their work, sometimes without charge.

The auction house usually reserves for itself the right to withdraw items from an auction without the consignor's permission, and without compensation to the consignor. This is rarely done, because no commissions are earned on withdrawn items. However, where there are questions of authenticity, an auction house may withdraw items rather than sell a fake.

Selling through an auction house does not always mean a traditional public auction, and auction houses sometimes act as dealers and make direct sales without catalogues and bidding by the public. Direct sales by auction houses are referred to as "private treaty" sales. Private treaties are appropriate where it is clear who the top buyers will be. Items are offered to these buyers with the consignor's consent, and a favorable sale is negotiated promptly. Overall commissions to the auction house tend to be lower for private treaty sales than full-fledged auction sales.

Timing and Location of Sale

Auction houses hold sales at different times of the year, sometimes in different locations. There are sales traditionally held in certain weeks, such as the Impressionist sales at Sotheby's and Christie's. Other sales are held in conjunction with shows or fairs, when dealers and collectors are in town and can attend in person. Timing can be crucial, not just because the markets in art and collectibles are so volatile, but also because it is best to sell when dealers and collectors can take notice and bid. This argues for placing your goods along with other similar items in sales featuring such items, such as selling Hawaiian stamps in a Hawaiian stamp sale. However, it occasionally happens that too many of a particular type of item in one sale may dilute bidding interest and result in lower prices.

The dominant market for fine art auctions in the United States is New York City, and with few exceptions, Sotheby's and Christie's hold their major sales there. Los Angeles, San Francisco, Santa Fe, Chicago, and Dallas are lesser art auction markets, and the rest of the country is developing slowly. This is likewise the case for rare stamps, which are generally auctioned in New York. For rare coins, major auctions take place nationwide. Leading firms such as Heritage Auctions hold major auctions during fairs such as the Long Beach Coin and Collectibles Expo and the Florida United Numismatists Convention. The largest rare coin auction of the year is generally held in conjunction with the American Numismatic Association's annual convention, which is held in a different city every year. For some types of art and collectibles, sales should be held outside the United States to reach the greatest number of bidders, and that is usually the case for specialized foreign art, antiquities, stamps, and coins.

Consignors have a limited influence on when and where their property is sold. Of course, consignment deadlines usually pass some months before a sale, so the timing of a consignor's contract determines which sales are still open. Beyond that, auction houses are quite candid when it comes to advising which sales would be best for particular material. The major art and collectibles auction houses have two tiers of sales, one in the main salesroom and one in a second space or on a different day. Heritage Auctions has live "Platinum Night" sales for the highest-value items, frequent "Signature" sales for middle-tier items, with weekly

Internet auctions rounding out the remainder. A single collector's consignment could include items of varying values, offered for sale in varying values. In exceptional cases, a collection is important enough to warrant a stand-alone auction with no items from any other consignors.

Commissions and Other Charges

For the consignor, the primary cost of selling at auction is the seller's commission, which is a percentage of the "hammer price" (winning bid) of each item. The seller's commission places the auction house's interests right alongside the consignor's, as increasing the hammer prices increases compensation to both. The amount of the seller's commission varies depending on the type of item and the value of the total consignment. For example, the usual "full" seller's commission for US rare coin sales is 10 percent to 17.5 percent of the hammer price, while for certain types of art or collectibles it may be as high as 25 percent (the higher the estimated value of a piece, the lower the seller's commission). However, auction houses are quite competitive with one another for major consignments, and as the value of the consignment increases, the consignor's ability to negotiate the commission rate downward improves, with no commission frequently available for larger consignments. Negotiating commission rates is beyond the scope of this book, but if you have a major consignment it is worth consulting an expert regarding which auction house(s) will best serve your needs and what commission rates might be available to you.

In addition to the seller's commission, auction houses charge buyers a commission, usually called a buyer's premium or buyer's fee (often abbreviated as BP), which ranges from 10 percent for online-only auctions to 20 percent or more depending on the auction house and the type of item being sold. This is where the auction house recoups its expenses and earns its profit, particularly where the seller's commission has been negotiated down to zero. Indeed, competitive auction houses sometimes offer consignors "negative commissions," meaning they share part of the BP with the consignor. Some auction houses have very consignor-friendly commission structures for as much as –10 percent, meaning the consignor would receive 100 percent of the hammer price plus another 10 percent coming out of the BP, with the auction house retaining the remainder of the BP.

Consignors should understand the impact of seller's commissions and BPs on their likely net proceeds from auction sales. A collector consigning a collectible with a fair market value of $10,000 might receive only $7,560 for it, based on a 10 percent seller's commission. As we'll see in the next chapter, a buyer wishing to pay approximately $10,000 for an item will bid no more than $8,400, taking into account the buyer's premium that will be added to the hammer price:

Hammer price	$8,400
Twenty percent buyer's premium	$1,680
Total proceeds	$10,080
Seller's commission	$840 (10 percent of hammer price)
Total commissions to auction house	$2,520
Net proceeds to consignor	$7,560

Don't let the above example scare you away from auctions, however. As discussed above, selling at auction not only increases greatly the likelihood that an item will sell at all, but also tends to maximize the selling price. It is frequently the case that items sell for considerably more than their estimated values at auction. And, as we've also seen, seller's commissions are negotiable where the consignment is of high value.

In addition to commissions, auction houses often require consignors to compensate them for certain additional out-of-pocket costs. One such cost is photography. Whether the auction is of Revolutionary War documents or movie posters, Rembrandts or animation art, the photographs contained in the auction catalogue are very important to mail (or Internet) bidders who cannot view the items personally prior to the sale. Quality photographs help the consignor by inviting more bids, thereby increasing activity on the item and, hopefully, increasing the price realized. Some auction houses use extremely high-quality color photographs for every item, others use photographs only for the most important items, and still others use no photographs at all. Photography costs are substantial, and some—though not all—auction houses will charge a fee of 1 percent to 2 percent of the hammer price to cover those costs. For large or important consignments, these charges are absorbed by the auction house. In any event, consignors should get an agreement (preferably in writing, as a rider to the consignment agreement) stating which items will be photographed, the size of the photographs, and whether they will appear alongside the item's written description in the catalogue or collectively with others elsewhere in the catalogue.

The second out-of-pocket expense some auction houses pass along to consignors is insurance. Major auction houses will insure items against loss or damage from the time they are shipped by the consignor to when the ultimate buyer picks them up after the sale. Make sure of this before you do business with an auction house. In some cases, the insured value is set by the consignor and in others, the insured value is simply fair market value. The consignment agreement usually provides that in the event of loss, the auction house will assign its rights under the policy to the consignor, in exchange for which the consignor releases the auction house from any liability. If the loss occurs after the sale, but before the buyer has picked up the item, the auction house will deduct its commission from the insurance proceeds before turning them over to the consignor. Consignors are entitled to see the insurance policy that will apply to their property. The usual insurance charge is also 1 percent to 2 percent of the hammer price, depending on the auction house and the type of item. Some auction houses absorb these costs on every item, others only with large consignments.

Advances

As has been discussed, there is generally a long period of time between when goods are consigned and when the consignor is paid for them after sale. As a convenience to consignors, auction houses usually offer what are called "advances." Advances are loans, with interest, payable from the proceeds of the sale. Generally, a large consignor can borrow 50 percent or more of the estimated value of the consignment. The major auction houses have affiliated financing companies that arrange advances, and the amounts can be quite significant.

The benefits of taking advances from an auction house are obvious—it puts cash into your pocket long before the auction, and auction houses are among the few people who will loan substantial amounts of money on the security of art and collectible objects. However, the interest rates can be high, although even these are negotiable in very large consignments (I've represented consignors who received interest-free advances from a major auction house). Remember that the auction house takes no legal risk in making advances—if the item does not sell at the auction, or sells for less than its estimated value, the consignor must still repay the entire advance. Overall, we don't recommend advances unless the terms are right and you really need cash before the sale.

If you do go ahead with an advance, you will be asked to sign a loan agreement and a security agreement, both of which will be on that auction house's standard printed form and will not (ordinarily) be negotiable. The agreements will authorize the auction house to subtract all amounts due on the loan from the proceeds of sale before paying the balance over to the consignor. They will provide that in the event that the items consigned sell for less than the amount due on the loan, you will promptly make up the difference. Also, they will provide that if the consigned items do not sell, they may be held as collateral by the auction house until the loan is repaid with interest.

Cataloguing

The auction house is responsible for preparing a catalogue describing all the lots in a sale, and mailing the catalogue to its list of potential bidders. In recent years, auction houses have placed their entire catalogues, including pictures and full item descriptions, online. In fact, online auction "catalogues" sometimes provide considerably more information than could be contained in a hard copy, by virtue of links to reference materials and to past sales of comparable items. Cataloguing is an important function, and how a lot is described in the catalogue can greatly affect both the number and amounts of bids received. Keep in mind that many bidders never see the items they bid on before the sale, and have only the catalogue descriptions (and photographs, if any) to go on.

Consignment agreements usually provide that the auction house has complete discretion with respect to all aspects of cataloguing. The first of these is lotting—that is, dividing the consignment into lots for sale. A painting, of course, will be a stand-alone lot, but it would not be unusual for a collection of two hundred common US and foreign stamps to be divided into fewer than ten lots, with the bulk of the material being grouped together into large lots. Do not expect that each and every item you consign will be a separate lot. Consignors who are unfamiliar with auction practices sometimes resent this, thinking that their "gems" aren't being properly handled. Remember that the auction house has every reason to want the items to sell for the highest possible price, and when making lotting decisions the auction house must balance the costs of individually lotting items with the benefits. In the stamp example above, individually lotting a large collection of foreign stamps will probably result in many lots going unsold because bidders simply aren't interested in bidding on them one at a time. It would also lengthen the auction tremendously and increase the auction house's costs for the auction. However, a large lot will sell to a collector or dealer who finds value in the group as a whole, and will save time and money for the auction house.

A second cataloguing decision about which the auction house has total discretion is lot numbering, meaning the order in which items are auctioned. This isn't as wide open as it may sound. Rare coins are almost always ordered by denomination, and by date within a particular denomination. Large cents come before twenty-cent pieces, and before silver dollars. Stamps are usually ordered by Scott catalogue number, US first followed by foreign in alphabetical (by country) order. While the sequence of lots of art were traditionally ordered chronologically and/or thematically, many auction houses now utilize their expertise and prioritize ordering in a way that maintains energy and excitement throughout the entire auction. As a consignor, it is worth knowing whether your item(s) will be sold at 7:00 pm on the first day of the auction or at 1:00 am on the third day. While mail and Internet bidders—particularly those in other time zones around the world—are just as active in the wee hours, floor bidders often are not.

The actual descriptions of the items are also ultimately in the auction house's sole discretion. For each item, the auction house's own staff, sometimes supplemented by renowned experts in specific fields, prepare a statement that may discuss authenticity, provenance, rarity, condition, and any special attributes or associations pertaining to an item. Here, every nuance can affect bidding. We have seen the legal difference between attributing a work of art to an artist or the "school" of the artist. Likewise, the use of phrases such as "best known" in describing an item might greatly influence bidders on that item. As a consignor, you have some right to know what the auction house plans to say about your property, and auction houses will sometimes (not often) offer to submit proposed lot descriptions to you to review. You may even be able to suggest changes and ask the auction house to add to, subtract from, or modify their descriptions. However, the final say lies with the auction house, whose reputation depends, in part, on the integrity and reliability of its lot descriptions. In addition to the *content* of the description, consignors occasionally negotiate the *size* of the space given to a particular lot. Regardless of the description itself, items that receive a full page in the catalogue attract more attention than those with only a few lines. This is another area where the market value of the item is important.

Consignor's Warranties

The consignment agreement will contain a warranty from the consignor regarding title to the goods being consigned. The purpose of this warranty is to enable the auction house to warrant title to the ultimate buyer. In New York, the law requires such a warranty, but even where no law requires a consignor's warranty of title an auction house will not accept a consignment without one. The warranty of title is in various parts, assuring the auction house that the consignor has sole title and power over the goods, that there are no liens or encumbrances over the goods, and that nobody else must consent to the auction sale of the goods. Heritage Auctions puts it as follows:

> You warrant that you are the sole owner of the Properties, that you have not encumbered the Properties in any way (by pledging the properties as collateral for a loan or in some other way), that you have the absolute right to consign the Properties to auction, that good title will pass to the purchaser, and that all of the Properties are genuine. If acting as agent for an undisclosed principal, you and your principal jointly and severally make all of the warranties and assume all of the obligations hereunder as though each of you were acting as the principal. You further warrant and agree to indemnify Auctioneer and hold Auctioneer harmless forever from and against any and all claims, demands, losses, liabilities, and expenses (including attorney fees) relating to the claim of breach of any of your representations and warranties, and an intended beneficiary of this warranty is the ultimate purchaser at auction and their transferees.

Generally, the consignment agreement does not require the consignor to make express or implied warranties regarding authenticity, condition/grade, or rarity. Consignors typically are not dealers, nor are they expected to be experts or to guarantee anything about their property. In fact, one reason collectors place property at auction is to have it examined and catalogued by the auction house's experts. As the next chapter will discuss, however, the auction house usually disclaims all such warranties to its buyers, and will accept returns from successful bidders if there is a dispute regarding the correctness of catalogue descriptions. In that event, the auction house may simply rescind the sale and return disputed items to the consignor, in effect requiring the consignor to back up the auction house's representations about the property.

ESTIMATES

The auction house is responsible for assigning estimates to each item. For art and most collectibles, auction catalogues include estimates but US rare coin auction catalogues often do not. Ordinarily, catalogue estimates are the auction house's good faith prediction of the selling price of the item. However, the auction house will usually err on the low side when making estimates, to stimulate mail and Internet bidding. Remember that bidders who do not view the lots in person prior to the sale rely entirely on the catalogue, and the higher the estimate, the fewer such bidders will take a chance and bid.

In 1996, Sotheby's auctioned property from the estate of Jacqueline Onassis, with items selling for many times the printed estimate. A footstool once used by Caroline Kennedy was estimated by Sotheby's at $100 to $150, and it hammered down for $29,000. A rocking chair once used by President Kennedy was estimated at $3,000 and sold for $475,000. Sotheby's extremely low estimates served three purposes. First, they reflected Sotheby's opinion—albeit disingenuous in this case—regarding the intrinsic value of each item, without the "Jackie" provenance. Second, they helped encourage more than 70,000 people to submit mail bids in the hope of acquiring something. Undoubtedly, there were many bidders on the rocking chair who would not have bothered had the estimate been in the $400,000 to $500,000 range. These bidders increased the national interest in what Sotheby's was doing, and by registering to bid they gave Sotheby's their contact information for Sotheby's to market to them in the future. Third, the low estimates made Sotheby's appear, at least to some, as having achieved miraculous results through their auctioneering skill. Auctioneers often promote themselves with examples of items selling at many times their estimates. Under the circumstances, and without any denigration of Sotheby's, the results of the Onassis sale speak more for the excitement of the buying public than for Sotheby's ability to outperform its estimates.

Consignors should review an auction house's estimates for its consigned items very carefully. In many cases, the auction house will discuss estimates before the consignment agreement has even been executed, and consignors should keep a record of those discussions lest the auction house attempt to lower them after the deal is done.

RESERVES

Estimates are very powerful tools in the auction business. However, in volatile markets such as art and collectibles, auction houses can be wrong in estimating value, and a consignor cannot assume that an item will not sell below the low estimate. If bidders are absent from the sale, worried about market trends, or just not interested in that item on that particular day, the lot will sell for the highest bid, however low that may be. To protect bidders from a bad market (or bad luck), auction houses allow consignors to establish reserve prices.

Reserves are confidential prices below which the lot cannot sell. They are set by the consignor, with input from the auction house, and the auction house prepares a written list of them with a copy for the consignor. Auction houses like to see reserves set no higher than 80 percent of the published estimate. At the auction, the auction house will open bidding, and will bid up to the reserve price (against the other mail and floor bidders) on behalf of the consignor. If other bidders do not outbid the reserve, the lot will be "bought in" and returned to the consignor.

For consignments containing many lots, reserving each lot individually can be an imperfect protection to consignors. Some lots might sell for less than their reserves, while others sell for many times the reserve. For consignors who merely want to assure themselves an *overall* minimum price, auction houses have increasingly been offering what is called a "floating reserve." Floating reserves allow the auction house to shift reserves from one lot to another. Where bidding on one item is brisk the reserve is increased, and for other lots it is lowered correspondingly.

The end result is that everything sells, and the consignor receives more than the minimum amount had the same total reserve been allocated differently.

Obviously, consignors do not consign property with the intent to buy them back. However, "buy-ins" are even more unhappy events for the auction house. The auction house has done all its cataloguing, advertising, and auctioneering, but without a sale it is deprived of a seller's commission as well as a buyer's premium. Therefore, auction houses usually require some compensation in the event that a consignor buys in his own property. That "buyback fee" is usually in the area of 5 percent of the reserve price. If the consignor actually bids on his or her property above the reserve price, most auction houses will treat the consignor as an ordinary buyer and charge the full buyer's fee (in New York, a consignor may not bid from the floor over the reserve, although he or she is free to do so as a mail or telephone bidder).

Under New York law, the high estimate for an item cannot be lower than the reserve price. This would effectively kill the chances of a remote (mail or Internet) bidder buying an item, and even floor bidders might be so influenced by the high estimate as to limit their bids to below the price at which the auction house is permitted to sell. This rule, which accords with long-standing policy at major auction houses, was imposed in part as a result of *Cristallina v. Christie's,*[1] a case involving a group of investors who consigned items to Christie's, some of which did not sell after having been reserved at prices substantially higher than Christie's published high estimates.

GUARANTEED MINIMUM PRICES

In larger consignments, auction houses sometimes guarantee that a certain sum will be realized by the consignor. This is different from a reserve, where failure to meet the consignor's expectations results in return of the property and a small fee to the auction house. With a guaranteed minimum price, the property is allowed to sell, but if the auction proceeds, after commissions, are less than the guaranteed amount, the auction house itself makes up the difference. In volatile markets, a consignor might want to know for certain what the consignment will

---

[1] Cristallina v. Christie's, 117 A.D.2d 284 (N.Y. App. Div. 1986).

bring months in the future. In addition, if the consignor is an estate or other fiduciary, guarantees eliminate the risk of market decline or some extraordinary event that keeps bidders from the auction.

Most major auction houses offer guarantees when competing for larger consignments, and some offer them to attract smaller lots as well. Consignors like to see auction houses put their own money where their estimates are. However, consignors do not always benefit from guarantees, and security has its price—auction houses usually adjust their commissions upward where there is a guarantee. Moreover, it simply is not true that whoever guarantees the most money will do the best job. Finally, guarantees and reserves are somewhat incompatible, because an auction house cannot be expected to meet a guaranteed amount if high consignor reserves result in many lots failing to sell. Therefore, consignors wanting the security of reserve prices on all lots may either have to give in on guarantees or allow the auction house to assist in setting reserves.

SETTLEMENT: TIMING AND PROCEDURE

In the auction business, payment of consignors and return of unsold property after the sale is called "settlement." The timing of settlement varies, but certain specific time periods tend to be used by the major auction houses. For example, Sotheby's and Christie's settle art and collectibles auctions thirty-five days after the date of sale, in accordance with New York's auctioneer regulations. In the rare coin field, forty-five days is standard.

Settlement dates allow auction houses a certain amount of "float." As will be noted in chapter 9, buyers must pay in full before taking delivery, and this usually happens promptly after a sale, particularly when the buyer is a dealer who plans on reselling the item. The auction house then has use of the funds for the remainder of the settlement period, without paying the consignor any interest. The expectation of prompt payment by buyers sometimes allows auction houses to commit to quicker settlement to a consignor in order to obtain a major consignment. We have seen auction houses offer to pay major consignors on the day of the auction, or even to deposit funds in an interest-bearing account in the consignor's name prior to the auction. Ordinarily, however, the time value of money during the settlement period is part of the auction house's compensation.

RISK OF NONPAYMENT BY THE BUYER

Despite the fact that most auction buyers pay quickly, *nonpayment* by the buyer is still a real risk for the consignor, particularly in volatile markets. For example, in April 1980, a major rare coin auction house faced defaults by numerous highly leveraged buyers who did not survive the steep drop in coin prices that month. If the buyer simply does not show up to claim the goods, the auction house will usually permit the consignor to place them in the next regularly scheduled sale, arrange a private treaty sale (perhaps to one of the underbidders), or return the item to the consignor.

It is, of course, possible for the consignor to sue the buyer for breach of contract, and in cases where the market has fallen since the auction it may be beneficial to do so, because the price bid at the auction will be greater than the fair market value of the item later on. Most consignors are surprised to learn, however, that the auction house is not responsible in nonpayment situations even when it delivers goods on credit to buyers who end up not paying for them. But this is generally the case in auction contracts. As in the case of an insurance loss, the auction house "assigns" its right to payment to the consignor, meaning that the consignor must make his claim directly against the delinquent buyer. Chapter 9 will discuss auction house credit arrangements. In collectibles auctions particularly, auction houses entice dealers to bid with thirty-day credit terms. Consignors would ordinarily be indifferent to such credit policies, expecting that they will get paid regardless of whether the successful buyer pays the auction house. But when shopping around a major consignment, make sure to confirm what credit arrangements will be available, and whether the auction house will protect the consignor against defaults by buying the items itself should the situation arise.

SUMMARY

Keep the following in mind when considering a possible auction consignment:

- Each area of art and collectibles has its own specialized auction houses, which can bring better results than "jacks of all trades."
- Speak to more than one auction company and have them send you sample consignment agreements and terms of sale.

- After you have discussed your property with each firm, get a written proposal from each.
- Be sure that the auction house explains the timing of the auction, its seller's and buyer's commissions, and any additional charges to you in connection with the consignment.
- Understand how your property will be described and estimated, and how reserves should be set.
- Ask how the auction house will advertise and market your property.
- If your consignment is substantial, nearly everything in the consignment agreement is negotiable.

9

Buying at Public Auction

Buying at a public auction is regulated by the terms and conditions of sale, a series of rules and regulations set forth in the auction catalogue (usually at the beginning of it), and occasionally supplemented at the commencement of the auction itself. This chapter will review the basic terms and conditions used by auction houses.

FLOOR BIDDING

Bidders who are physically present in the sales room during the auction are called "floor bidders." The popular image of bidders raising their paddles (or twitching their noses) to be recognized by the auctioneer stems from the traditional floor bidding situation. Technology has expanded the concept of the sales "room," however. In the 1990s, auction houses introduced the concept of simulcast auctions, where floor bidders in multiple locations could bid against one another, each being recognized by an auctioneer in the room with them. Over time, these simulcast auctions reached more distant locations, although for reasons of practicality the norm remains a single live auction setting with remote bidders on the telephone or at their computers bidding online. Most major auction houses permit bidders to bid by telephone. Doing so requires a bidder to maintain a live telephone connection with the auction sales room, speaking with a member of the auction house staff who relays the bids on particular items. Such bidders are, in effect, bidding from the floor, because they have complete control over whether to bid and how much to bid, just as though they were in the room physically. This likewise is the case with Internet bidding, which usually is permitted all the way through to the final fall of the auctioneer's hammer, although in some cases will commence a week or two before the live session and be closed when the live session is about to start.

Floor bidding also includes those who are represented on the floor by agents. This is a common practice at art and collectibles auctions, and dealers often represent their collector clients for a commission. Bidding through an agent saves the collector the costs of attending an auction that the dealer-agent would be attending anyway. It also enables the collector to employ the dealer's expertise to avoid purchasing the wrong items or overpaying. The commission is sometimes a small price to pay for this kind of "on the spot" backup. However, unlike the telephone bidder, bidders who employ agents are giving up a certain amount of control over the bidding process. A prudent bidder will set dollar limits on how much the agent can bid, but within those parameters the bidder is trusting the agent to make the right decision with respect to his or her money. He or she is not there when the lot is opened for bids and can't amend the agent's instructions.

New York's auctioneer regulations (discussed in detail later in this chapter) prohibit consignors from bidding over their reserves from the floor. Presumably this is intended to discourage consignors from "bidding up" others on the floor who don't realize that they own the property being offered.

BIDDER REGISTRATION AND CREDIT ARRANGEMENTS

To bid at an auction, a buyer must be registered with the auction house. This consists of filling out a form and receiving a bidder number (printed on a "paddle"). Auction houses will require certain information from bidders, including name, address, and telephone number, and may in some cases ask for a Social Security Number or driver's license information.

Where a bidder expects to bid large sums and he is unknown to the auction house, it makes sense to advise the auctioneer in advance and be approved for credit. Armen did this early in his career before bidding $250,000 on a rare coin on behalf of a client at a New York auction. Auction houses reserve the right to reject any bid made from the floor (or in any other manner), and all the major auction houses have stories of people bidding huge amounts for works of art and turning out to be penniless. However, even persons well known to the auction house can default on their purchases which, as discussed in the previous chapter, can affect settlement to the consignor.

ABSENTEE BIDDING

Most bidders cannot physically attend auctions, however, or even attend them virtually by being available by telephone or Internet in real time during the live bidding sessions. These absentee bidders bid by mail or on the Internet. Absentee bidding is encouraged by auction houses, both to give out of towners the ability to buy items and to create more competition for floor bidders and thereby increase the prices realized. Mail or Internet bidders receive the auction catalogue and rely on the lot descriptions in the catalogue, or on physical inspection of lots during viewing, or both. They provide "max" bids—the most they are prepared to pay for the item—and their bids are recorded by auction house staff who then announce them at the sale as though the bidder were there.

Absentee bidding, at first blush, seems quite risky, in that the bidder has nothing but the auctioneer's estimates and his or her own value information on which to base his or her bids. Many people think that if they bid ten thousand dollars for an item that's how much they will pay, even if the highest other bid is one thousand dollars. This is untrue. Most auction houses would award the mail bidder the lot for the next increment over one thousand dollars.

Another myth about absentee bidding is that sales are final. As discussed more elsewhere in this chapter, in many cases an absentee bidder who has not inspected the lot he or she purchased has greater rights than would a floor bidder.

WARRANTY OF TITLE

Auction houses do not make many warranties to buyers. This is not illogical, because (normally) the auction house does not own the items it sells and is not, strictly speaking, the "seller." However, auction houses act as agent for the sellers—their consignors. Bidders at auction do not know the consignors and cannot negotiate directly with consignors what warranties will accompany the goods on which they bid. Moreover, an auction house's commissions, including the buyer's premium, are in part a recognition of its expertise in authenticating and appraising the items it sells. Every day, items that might have sold for less elsewhere benefit from the increased confidence buyers have in purchasing from a major auction house. It is fair to say that auction buyers have certain expectations about items they purchase at one of the "majors." Expectations, however, do not always translate into legal rights. The Uniform Commercial Code (UCC), which provides so many protections to ordinary retail buyers, does not apply to auction sales. Instead, what rights auction buyers have are set forth in the terms and conditions of sale prepared by the auction house and set forth in the auction catalogue.

Buyers at auction nearly always receive a warranty of title, and that is required in certain states (such as New York). The previous chapter discussed how auction houses require consignors to give them a warranty of title, and to indemnify and hold harmless the auction house in the event that the consignor's title to an item is challenged by someone else. The consignor's warranty and hold harmless agreement enables the auction house, in turn, to warrant title to the buyer. In some instances, such as sales of art or collectibles seized by the Internal Revenue Service (IRS) for nonpayment of taxes, even that warranty is not given, because peculiar IRS regulations permit delinquent taxpayers to pay the outstanding taxes and reclaim their property until the very moment that the successful bidder pays for it after the auction. This, of course, sometimes chills the bidding at such sales.

DISCLAIMER OF OTHER WARRANTIES

Beyond the warranty of title, there is little else that an auction house legally stands behind. Despite the extensive catalogue descriptions, and an auction house's centuries-old history, reading the terms and conditions of sale is a lesson in how to disclaim just about all responsibility to buyers in a retail sale of art or collectibles. Here is a typical disclaimer from a Heritage Auctions "Terms and Conditions of Auction" for an art auction:

> NO WARRANTY, WHETHER EXPRESSED OR IMPLIED, IS MADE WITH RESPECT TO ANY DESCRIPTION CONTAINED IN THIS AUCTION OR ANY SECOND OPINE. Any description of

merchandise or second opine contained in this Auction is for the sole purpose of identifying merchandise for those Bidders who do not have the opportunity to view merchandise prior to bidding, and no description of merchandise has been made part of the basis of the bargain or has created any express warranty that merchandise would conform to any description made by Auctioneer. Color variations can be expected in any electronic or printed imaging, and are not grounds for the return of any lot. NOTE: Auctioneer, in specified auction venues, e.g. Fine Art, may have express written warranties and Bidder is referred to those specific terms and conditions.

. . .

FINE & DECORATIVE ARTS TERM A: LIMITED WARRANTY: Auctioneer warrants authorship, period or culture of each lot sold in this catalog as set out in the **BOLD**-face type heading in the catalog description of the lot, with the following exclusions. This warranty does not apply to:

i. authorship of any paintings, drawings or sculpture created prior to 1870, unless the lot is determined to be a counterfeit which has a value at the date of the claim for rescission which is materially less than the purchase price paid for the lot; or
ii. any catalog description where it was specifically mentioned that there is a conflict of specialist opinion on the authorship of a lot; or
iii. authorship which on the date of sale was in accordance with the then generally accepted opinion of scholars and specialists, despite the subsequent discovery of new information, whether historical or physical, concerning the artist or craftsman, his students, school, workshop or followers; or
iv. the identification of periods or dates of execution which may be proven inaccurate by means of scientific processes not generally accepted for use until after publication of the catalog, or which were unreasonably expensive or impractical to use at the time of publication of the catalog.

The term counterfeit is defined as a modern fake or forgery, made less than fifty years ago with the intent to deceive. The authenticity of signatures, monograms, initials, or other similar indications of authorship is expressly excluded as a controlling

> factor in determining whether a work is a counterfeit under the meaning of these Terms and Conditions of Auction.
>
> . . .
>
> FINE & DECORATIVE ARTS TERM F: Any claim as to authorship, provenance, authenticity, or other matter under the remedies provided in the Fine Arts Terms and Conditions or otherwise must be first transmitted to Auctioneer by credible and definitive evidence within the applicable claim period. Auctioneer, in processing the written claim, may require the Purchaser to obtain the written opinion of two recognized experts in the field who are mutually accepted by Auctioneer and Purchaser. Upon receipt of the two opinions, Auctioneer shall determine whether to rescind the sale. The Purchaser's claim must be presented in accord with the remedies provided herein and is subject to the limitations and restrictions provided (including within the described time limitations). Regardless of Purchaser's submissions there is no assurance after such presentment that Auctioneer will validate the claim. Authentication is not an exact science and contrary opinions may not be recognized by Auctioneer. Even if Auctioneer agrees with the contrary opinion of such authentication and provides a remedy within these Terms and Conditions or otherwise, our liability for reimbursement for bidder's third party opines shall not exceed $500. The right of rescission, return, or any other remedy provided in these Terms and Conditions, or any other applicable law, does not extend to authorship of any lot which at the date of Auction was in accordance with the then generally accepted opinion of scholars and specialists, despite the subsequent discovery of new information, whether historical or physical, concerning the artist, his students, school, workshop or followers. Purchaser by placing a bid expressly waives any claim or damage based on such subsequent information as described herein. It is specifically understood that any refund agreed to by the Auctioneer would be limited to the purchase price.
>
> FINE & DECORATIVE ARTS TERM G: Provenance and authenticity, excluding attributions in **BOLD**-face type, are guaranteed by neither the consignor nor Auctioneer. While every effort is made to determine provenance and authenticity, it is the responsibility of the Bidder to arrive at their own conclusion prior to bidding.

The disclaimers of Sotheby's, Christie's, and the other major auction houses are essentially identical.

The UCC protects buyers from problems relating to authenticity and Heritage's above disclaimer of that warranty for older works. Even with newer works, however, the terms of Heritage's disclaimer protect Heritage and its consignors from the types of claims that have been discussed with retailers. Recall the Mary Cassatt painting that Sotheby's sold in 1987 (discussed in chapter 3). After a Cassatt authentication committee was created in 1990, it declared the work a forgery, and when the buyer approached Sotheby's in 1993 to sell the painting as part of a larger consignment, Sotheby's was reluctant to do so in light of the cloud on authenticity. The buyer sued, and Sotheby's refused to refund the buyer's original $632,500 purchase price on the basis of the five-year limitation period. The parties reached an amicable settlement in early 1996.

An even more startling example of the auction buyer's quandary is the case of a collector who bought a Faberge egg at a Christie's sale. Concerned that the egg was not genuine, he claimed a right of return and refused to pay Christie's. Christie's, assuring him of the egg's genuineness, sued to collect the hammer price and buyer's fee, and arranged for a written statement from a renowned Faberge egg expert that the egg was genuine. The collector agreed to pay for the egg, as well as for Christie's legal fees. After having the egg in his safe deposit box for a few years, the collector consigned it to Christie's for sale. Christie's refused to accept the egg, doubting its genuineness. The same expert who had earlier said the egg was genuine now said he was not sure. The collector sued Christie's, and the case was eventually settled. And a collector who bought an 1848 painting attributed to George Inness in a 1987 Sotheby's sale, and who learned authoritatively in 1995 that the painting was not by Inness, blamed Sotheby's and picketed in front of Sotheby's New York offices.

In rare coin and stamp sales, buyers generally may return lots that are counterfeit. Chapter 3 mentions that the leading association of professional coin dealers, the Professional Numismatists Guild (PNG), requires its members to guarantee authenticity. In the increasingly limited field of rare stamp auction houses, it is typical to permit buyers of uncertified stamps to have them examined by independent experts after purchase, and to have a right of return should the expert determine that the stamp is not genuine, or has been altered.

There is, of course, no ideal way to apportion the authenticity risk in auction situations between consignor, auction house, and buyer, so the approach of the major auction houses is as good as any. As a buyer, make sure you understand where the risk lies with your purchases.

With respect to grading or quality issues, the typical auction house terms and conditions provide even fewer rights. For example, in art auctions returns are only allowed in the case of items acknowledged to be counterfeit. In rare coin and stamp auctions, mail bidders may return lots for reasons of quality within a short time after receipt, generally three to five days. Even this right is sometimes lost with items carrying third-party certificates (the presumption being that mail bidders cannot disagree with the grades of certified coins or stamps), and usually there are no rights of return for floor bidders, who are assumed to have inspected the lots before bidding.

BUYER'S PREMIUM AND PAYMENT TERMS

The last chapter introduced the terms "hammer price" and "buyer's premium." The hammer price, of course, is the highest bid recorded for an item, which determines the successful bidder. However, buyers at auction must not forget about the buyer's premium, and should take it into account when deciding how much to bid. For example, if a buyer attends an auction with a 20 percent buyer's premium and wants to pay no more than $10,000 for an item, the highest bid should be approximately $8,400, because should that bid be successful your total cost (hammer price + buyer's premium) will be $10,080.

Generally speaking, successful bidders at public auction must claim their items promptly and make payment. Auction houses do not extend credit, except to the extent that they accept a personal check for payment. Bidders expecting to pay substantial amounts at an auction should contact the auction house in advance to discuss payment arrangements.

PERILS OF FLOOR BIDDING

The basics of bidding at auction are easy to understand, but there are certain subtle ways in which an unwary bidder might be manipulated by others in the room into overpaying for particular items. It's a good idea for less-experienced collectors and investors to use the catalogue estimates as a guide, and to enter the auction with a fixed dollar limit on each and every item on which one plans to bid. Otherwise, some of the following practices could hurt.

The atmosphere in an auction room can sometimes be quite feverish, and it is easy to spend more than planned, even without outside help. But consignors to auctions sometimes take advantage of inexperienced persons by bidding on their own property. Without knowing that the competing bidder is the consignor, a bidder might take such bids as validation of his or her view of the item's value, thus resulting in even higher bids. Of course, the consignor will not be the high bidder in such situations, but the bids will increase what the unwary buyer has to pay. New York City's auction regulations prohibit floor bidding by consignors, but the practice is not illegal in any other state or city. Even in New York, the consignor can submit a mail bid for his own property at auction.

POOLING

Bid rigging, or "pooling," consists of collusion between bidders at auction which lessens competition otherwise to be expected between them. While its most significant public impact is with the sale of public contracts, the government and private parties have brought actions to restrain and/or penalize bid rigging in a number of private contexts as well, including art and collectibles auctions. Pooling can be attractive to buyers who don't understand that it is illegal. For example, if three similar items are being offered at an antiquities auction and three bidders are interested, it would make sense for the three to agree that only one of them will bid on each item. Each gets what he wants without having to bid against the others. Of course, from the government's standpoint, the result is an artificially low hammer price. Not only is pooling a violation of the Sherman Antitrust Act of 1890, it is a per se violation, meaning that once a pooling agreement has been found, the government does not have to show that prices were actually affected by the pooling. In other words, in the example above, it would not be a defense that the presence of other buyers at the auction caused the three items to sell for their fair market value anyway.

In *United States v. Ronald Pook,*[1] antique dealers were prosecuted for pooling at antique auctions. The court noted that the Sherman Act had

---

[1] United States v. Ronald Pook, Crim. No. 87-274, 1988 U.S. Dist. LEXIS 3398 (E.D. Pa. Apr. 18, 1988).

never been applied to antique auctions, but that "the same rules against agreements to restrain price competition apply to all economic areas." The court stated that "Consignors and auctioneers were invariably deprived by members of the pool of their proper share of the ultimate sales prices of items purchased at public auctions and sold later at private auctions." Defendants' convictions were affirmed. More recently, the Department of Justice Antitrust Division announced guilty pleas in a case involving pooling at an auction of rare bank notes at Christie's in New York.

NEW YORK'S AUCTION REGULATIONS

Many states and cities impose some sort of license requirement on auctioneers for the protection of the public who buy at auction, but only New York City, where the vast majority of art and collectibles (by dollar volume) are auctioned, regulates the auction process itself. New York's regulations are administered by the Department of Consumer Affairs and are available to the public. Their purpose is, with one exception, to protect people who buy at auction, and therefore it applies more to the terms and conditions of sale discussed in this chapter than to consignment agreements.

The regulations are, basically, disclosure requirements. Auction houses are supposed to disclose, among other things, whether they have an interest in certain items, whether they have loaned money to consignors or buyers, that there are reserves on certain items, that the auction house may bid for its own account or permit consignors to do so. Either each affected lot has a statement in its catalogue description (i.e., "this lot is owned by the auction house"), or the lot description includes a symbol that, when translated, amounts to the same disclosure. Some auction houses say in so many words "some lots may be owned by the auction house and this statement is deemed to be in every lot description," which probably isn't enough.

Not all auctions are subject to the Auction Regulations, because of Regulation 28, which states that the regulations relating to disclosure of auction house interest and the consignor's buyback rights do not apply where a written catalogue containing precise, detailed lot descriptions is available for a reasonable period of time prior to the auction, the values of lots can be determined using standard recognized reference sources, and sales are not final until the buyer has a chance to verify that the lot was as it was described. All those characteristics apply to auctions by the major art and collectibles auctioneers. Where every lot in a sale or portion of a sale is reserved, you may see a simple statement on the title page for that portion so stating. It is not sufficient to generalize in the terms and conditions that "some items might carry reserves." Sotheby's uses a ■ to mark reserved items, and Christie's uses a ● symbol before each lot number to signify that the lot carries a reserve.

New York prohibits certain auction house practices that have caused problems in the past, unless the right to do so is specifically disclosed in the terms and conditions. Among these are loaning money to bidders, using inside information to bid on items for the auction house's own account, and making consecutive bids up to the reserve price. We're not happy with these practices anyway, and most reputable auction houses do not do them. The only unusual requirement is that a consignor can't bid from the floor over his own reserve price, although he can bid by mail or by phone. Usually, the problem of consignors bidding up their own property is addressed by the auctioneer announcing that the consignor is bidding, but in New York there is an outright prohibition.

SUMMARY

Remember the following when bidding (and hopefully buying!) in a public auction:

- Read the terms and conditions of the sale to know the specific terms (including costs and who bears the risk of authenticity) of the auction.
- Warranties are often disclaimed in terms and conditions (the auction house doesn't own the item, after all), but items sold at auction have been examined by auction house professionals which decreases some concerns requiring warranties.
- Remember you must register as a bidder before the auction begins and, if the auction includes high-value items, be prepared to provide identification such as a social security or driver's license number.
- If you are unable to attend an auction in person, you usually have the option to place real-time bids online or over the telephone,

or may commission a dealer to act as your agent and attend in your place.

- Many auction houses also allow absentee bidding, where you tell the auction house the maximum amount you'll pay for the item and the auction house will incorporate you as a bidder unless the bidding surpasses your maximum.
- Coordinating your bidding with other bidders in the auction (even those who are bidding on a different item than you are) often qualifies as illegal "pooling."
- Certain states, like New York, have additional protections for bidders, such as prohibiting consignors from placing bids on their own items to drive up the price and requiring the auction house to disclose if they have an ownership interest in the item.

PART 3
Buying and Selling Art and Collectibles Remotely

The amazing expansion of online commerce has impacted the art and collectibles markets, perhaps more slowly than other niche areas, but significantly, nonetheless. Twenty years ago, it was nearly inconceivable that someone would trust an online seller, perhaps operating only under an alias (username) and without a posted physical address, to deliver an artwork or collectible paid for in advance. Such transactions, if they occurred, were for unimportant items at low prices. In other words, the online art and collectibles marketplace did not compete with the conventional one, but merely filled out its bottom layer. All this has changed. Today, everyone's access to the Internet serves the industry in both providing brick-and-mortar dealers and auction houses with other channels to sell goods and enabling purely online operators to reach buyers and sellers as has never happened before. The online art and collectibles universe borrows heavily from the legal structures described above but has its own rules and regulations as well.

10

Basics of Buying and Selling Collectibles Online

The Internet has enabled collectors to cut out the middleman—that is, to buy and sell their collection without engaging (and paying commission to) a dealer. Even the online auction houses frequently have lower fees than traditional auction houses that have to cover the expenses of live viewings and auctions. While art collectors have been more reluctant to participate in online transactions than those interested in collectibles, as Internet sales become more commonplace and regulated, more and more art collectors are venturing online.

24/7 ACCESS TO (NOT ALWAYS GOOD) INFORMATION

The Internet is amazing, but not always in a good way. Consumers can buy nearly anything they desire from their living rooms, and compare vendors by price, reputation, location, and so on. However, in a consumer's living room all vendors might appear alike, and reputations cannot be checked easily. Price, availability, and reliability are difficult to verify. And perhaps most importantly, online testimonials and customer "feedback" can be manipulated to make unscrupulous dealers seem on par with the best in the business.

Using one example from the coin collectibles marketplace, the busy market in modern precious metal coins as individual retirement account (IRA) investments has spawned a slew of "independent" review sites, which claim to compare coin dealers impartially to assist investors. Some of these sites review dealers individually, others show side-by-side comparisons using various criteria, and still others involve video presentations by so-called investment advisors about precious metal investing, leading to a discussion of dealers from which to buy.

While these sites—which exist not only for coins but for just about every other form of collectible—look like useful tools for investors, in fact the reviewers tend to not be independent, but rather compensated by the dealers they recommend. One California precious metals retailer stands out as the one recommended by nearly every review site. Currently, there are several lawsuits against that dealer complaining that its network of review sites violates both a Federal Trade Commission (FTC) rule and California statutory law.

The FTC "Disclosure of Material Connections" rule, codified at 16 C.F.R. 255.5, states "When there exists a connection between the endorser and the seller of the advertised product that might materially affect the weight or credibility of the endorsement (i.e., the connection is not reasonably expected by the audience), such connection must be fully disclosed." A review site that claims to be independent, but which is compensated solely by the one coin dealer it always recommends, violates that rule.

Of course, just because a reviewer doesn't disclose its sponsor relationships doesn't make the reviews fraudulent. Like an athlete who actually uses the sports drink he promotes, someone can be paid for telling the truth. Unfortunately, most of these IRA investment review sites go way beyond the truth, or even an average consumer's credence. For example, one site faults coin dealers who have spotless records with their local Better Business Bureaus, speculating that they could have paid an organization to erase complaints, or changed their company names after excessive complaints had been filed. Others, more insidiously, mislead consumers into clicking on links that send their personal information, including name, email address, and phone number to their sponsoring dealer when it appears the viewer is clicking a link to another page on the reviewer's website. The consumer then gets a barrage of sales calls from the sponsor.

Fraudulent activity such as the above constitutes common law fraud and violations of applicable unfair business practice and false advertising laws, and possibly also state or federal laws prohibiting telemarketing fraud.

The numismatic marketplace provides a great deal of information about dealers. Consumers can determine whether a dealer is a member of the Professional Numismatists Guild (PNG) or the American Numismatic Association (ANA), whether it is an authorized dealer of the major grading services, and whether it advertises in *Coin World*, for just a few indicia of longevity, stature, and reliability. Don't rely on Internet review sites to make the important decisions about where to buy coins.

COMMON PRACTICES FOR ONLINE SALES PLATFORMS

Many different types of sales platforms have sprung up on the Internet. This section provides an overview of the process of a few types of sales platforms.

eBay, of course, is one of the best known, allowing individuals to auction off their items. While under limited conditions eBay allows users to make purchases without an account, if you want to place bids and utilize other services of eBay, you'll need to create an account. eBay allows for three different types of transactions:

1. **Auction**—The seller may list a starting price and a length of time to leave the bidding open (usually several days) and interested buyers can enter a bid that exceeds the starting price. Bidders can monitor and continue to enter bids as the price rises (you've likely heard of bid "snipers" who place a winning bid at the last seconds before the auction closes). However, bidders can also enter their maximum bid at one time and not have to monitor several days of bidding. Once the maximum bid is entered, eBay will continue to automatically enter bids on your behalf until the price exceeds your maximum bid. Sellers benefit from this process as well, because increased frequency of bidding drives up the ultimate hammer price.
2. **Buy It Now**—In addition to open bidding on an item, a seller can list a flat price they will accept. For example, at the time of

writing this section, a comic book is listed with a starting bid of $9,500 and a "buy it now" price of $12,500. This can lead to faster sales rather than waiting for bidding to continue for another four days. However, the "buy it now" price is the maximum price the item will sell for, since the moment the bidding approaches that price, someone can instead buy it and cut the bidding short.

3. **Best Offer**—The buyer can send the seller an offer directly. This is at the buyer's option, usually where the buyer thinks the starting bid is overpriced (which can also become apparent if the bidding is almost closed and the item has received no bids).

Of course, one of the disadvantages of taking the "DIY" route to buy and sell your collectibles is that there is no expert from the auction house reviewing and giving an estimated value for the items, resulting in collectors overstating starting prices.

No experts (and generally lower overhead costs) does come with its advantages: lower fees. As discussed elsewhere in this book, traditional auction houses are moving away from charging seller's fees, relying more and more on the fees paid by buyers alone. Many online auction houses are following the trend, with competitive buyer's fees of 10 percent to 12 percent. eBay is the exception, where only the sellers pay a fee, in the form of a percentage of the sales price realized for each item. Fees on eBay usually range between 12 percent and 15 percent of the sales price up to $7,500 and then a reduced 2 percent to 7 percent on the portion in excess of $7,500. Non-fungible tokens (NFTs) sell at a flat rate of 5 percent.

eBay usually does not take possession of the items offered for sale (and therefore does not have the ability to review the quality of the item or accuracy of the description), but it does have a guarantee policy that eBay will pay the refund if a customer receives an item that does not conform to the description or pictures. eBay will then pursue the seller for reimbursement.

Other online forums that facilitate sales but do not take possession of the items themselves do not have a guaranty or refund policy; any dispute is left to the individual buyer and seller to resolve (or not). While it's understandable that a company would not want to take on the liability of a guaranty when they do not have an opportunity to examine the item, the purchase is less secure. Vetting the seller individually then becomes more significant.

When buying online, either through an auction or other sales platforms such as those described in this chapter, buyers should identify first who is responsible for holding and shipping the item, and second, who you can pursue for a refund if the item is not as described.

While eBay offers "DIY" auctions and sales of all categories of art and collectibles (and other goods), there are many category-specific (comic books, sports, coins, etc.) collector forums that also provide for transactions between members, such as certifiedcoinexchange.com and ha.com.

The Certified Coin Exchange (CCE) is an online platform for coin dealers to list and trade coins. Although this platform charges membership fees, it also compiles price guides and recent sales, allowing dealers to generate some of the most current price estimates for coins available. CCE is only open to dealers so, unlike eBay, collectors must consign to a dealer to sell through CCE, but doing so brings the dealer expertise and customers that may result in higher prices than selling on one's own.

Forums such as ha.com (which primarily operates Heritage Auctions) encourage members to post images and descriptions of all items in their collection, whether or not they're currently looking to sell them, just to share and discuss. However, other members can also make an offer to purchase any item at any time (though the current owner doesn't have to accept the offer!). Like ha.com, some of these forums are owned and hosted by an auction house or collectibles dealer, who then can review the postings you've made of your collection to see how significant of a collector (and therefore potential customer of theirs) you are. However, there are also benefits to the potential customer in that situation because if they choose to offer an item for sale or auction, much of the information about the piece has already been shared.

ENFORCEABLE ONLINE AGREEMENTS

Everyone who even owns a phone or computer is aware of the various "terms and conditions of use" that show up in the fine print at the bottom of most web pages or that pop up when you install an app. Whether you're participating on a website or looking to operate one, knowing what makes website agreements enforceable (as well as what unique terms you may find relating to art or collectibles) is vital.

This section primarily addresses how someone operating a website can set up their terms and conditions (and any other agreement pertaining to the website and its services) in a manner that they will be able to enforce against visitors to the website later. But for those visiting a website, even if the website would not be able to enforce its terms and conditions against you (perhaps you didn't see them at the time of your purchase), if you believe they are in your favor (such as a risk of loss provision, see chapter 13), you can always enforce the terms and conditions against the website operator.

Knowledge is the key factor in whether an agreement is or is not enforceable. And by "knowledge," we mean knowledge that there *are* terms and conditions, not necessarily knowledge of what those terms and conditions are. Courts across the country have held that if a person visits a website and has knowledge that there are terms and conditions, they will be bound to those terms and conditions, whether or not they chose to follow the link and actually read them.

But how to prove that the visitor had knowledge? Many webmasters place a link to the terms and conditions at the bottom of the web page and assume they're all set. The actual terms and conditions state that anyone visiting the website agrees to the terms and conditions just by visiting the website. After all, if someone admits they were on the website they were looking at the screen, right? Wrong.

This is generally referred to as a "browsewrap" agreement, where someone browsing a web page would see a link to terms and conditions; such an agreement is often unenforceable. Because the terms and conditions of a website are usually at the bottom of the page and require the person viewing the site to actively scroll to the bottom of the page, courts generally want proof that the visitor did actually scroll all the way down to the bottom and that the link to the terms and conditions was sufficiently large and visible that someone who was just browsing the site (and not looking specifically for the terms and conditions) would notice it.

For example, in 2014, the Ninth Circuit Court of Appeals reviewed the case *Nguyen v. Barnes & Noble, Inc.*[1] Nguyen sued Barnes & Noble for deceptive business practices and false advertising concerning the availability of items offered in a "fire sale." Barnes & Noble moved to compel

[1] Nguyen v. Barnes & Noble, Inc., 763 F.3d 1171 (2014).

arbitration pursuant to its website terms and conditions. However, the terms and conditions were a link at the bottom of the page and the Ninth Circuit affirmed the lower court's ruling that Nguyen could not be bound to the terms and conditions because there was no evidence that he had known they were there.

The most common situation where a browsewrap agreement has been enforced is where there was an ongoing violation and the website owner contacted the violator directly with a cease and desist letter that the violator then ignored. In 2007, Southwest Airlines sued Boardfirst, a company attempting to profit from circumventing Southwest's "first to check in, first to board" policy. After purchasing a ticket to fly on Southwest, which did not assign a seat, the passenger had to then check in through the Southwest website within the twenty-four hours prior to the flight itself, and would receive a boarding group A, B, or C. The earliest to check in therefore became the first to board and select their seats. Boardfirst was a company that, for a fee, would take the passenger's information and, using automatic functions similar to those used in website scraping, would check in exactly when the twenty-four-hour period began. Southwest argued that Boardfirst's service was a violation of the terms and conditions, which prohibited both robotic activity on the website and logging in under someone else's account. The terms and conditions were only located as a link at the bottom of the Southwest website. However, while Southwest couldn't prove that Boardfirst knew of the terms and conditions when it began operating, Southwest did send a cease and desist letter, which Boardfirst ignored. Because Boardfirst continued its operations after receiving a cease and desist letter from Southwest, the court ruled that Boardfirst's subsequent access of the website was pursuant to the terms and conditions.[2]

Instead of a browsewrap agreement, a better alternative is referred to as a "clickwrap" agreement. A clickwrap agreement requires a user to check a box or click an icon to signify agreement with the terms and conditions before they are allowed to complete certain transactions or view protected content. Think of an app that has a pop-up statement that "use of this app constitutes agreement to the Terms & Conditions," which the user has to click "agree" to move past, or the final page in a

---

[2] Southwest Airlines Co. v. Boardfirst, LLC, Case No. 3:06-CV-0891-B (N.D. Tex. Sept. 12, 2007).

website account setup that says "by clicking confirm you agree to the Terms & Conditions."

Even where the terms themselves actually appear in a separate hyperlinked web page but where language accompanying the box or icon indicates that checking the box or clicking the icon indicates assent to such terms, courts usually enforce these agreements.

In *Swift v. Zynga Game Network, Inc.*,[3] the court found that a hyperlink to the terms of services that appeared right below an "Accept" button—along with a statement that clicking "Accept" meant the user accepted the terms—was sufficient to prove the user agreed to those terms. Even if the user didn't follow the link and read the terms and conditions, they knew they were entering into the agreement and could have read the terms and conditions if they wanted to.

But even with a clickwrap agreement, the language must be clear that the user is agreeing to the terms and conditions when they click their consent. In *Holdbrook Pediatric Dental, LLC, v. Pro Computer Service, LLC*,[4] the defendant's service agreement was available on its website, where the page contained a hyperlink to the terms and conditions, and a link to download the service agreement to sign and return. The fact that the terms and conditions were only available via the online hyperlink and the consent was only possible through an ink-on-paper signature had no significance to the court. The court acknowledged that the service agreement could incorporate the terms and conditions via the hyperlink, but that Pro Computer fell short of doing so in this instance. The fact that there was a hyperlink to the terms and conditions was insufficient to incorporate them into the agreement because there was no language to that effect, such as "by signing this agreement, signor consents to the terms & conditions."

These decisions all ultimately show that enforcing terms and conditions comes down to whether or not you can prove someone knew the terms and conditions applied to them. A clickwrap agreement provides an easier method for a website to create a record that the user saw the terms and conditions and knew they were agreeing to be bound to them.

---

[3] Swift v. Zynga Game Network, Inc., 805 F. Supp. 2d 904 (N.D. Cal. 2011).

[4] Holdbrook Pediatric Dental, LLC, v. Pro Computer Service, LLC, Case No. 14-6115 (N.J. July 21, 2015).

SUMMARY

When buying or selling art and collectibles online, remember:

- Utilize industry associations and the major grading/authentication services to vet dealers rather than rely on review sites that may have been paid or falsified their experience.
- When choosing how to sell your items online, review the policies to know what additional responsibilities the seller bears that would traditionally be handled by the auction house.
- Websites can enforce their terms and conditions by proving that you knew there were terms and conditions (usually you check a box when you create an account), regardless of whether you chose to read them.

11

Copyright Considerations When Displaying Art and Collectibles Online

Artworks are creative works usually qualifying for copyright protection. Even collectibles often carry some copyrights as to a design or photograph. Copyrights are primarily the rights to control who sells, publishes, and reproduces a creative work. However, these intangible copyrights in a creative work are not inseparable from the physical (or electronic) piece that may be sold.

Congress provides not only many rights but also support to copyright owners in enforcing their rights against infringers, especially for those who register their copyright with the US Copyright Office. See chapter 16 for more detail on resolving disputes over copyrights.

OWNERSHIP OF COPYRIGHTS

Buyers of original works of art sometimes think they are acquiring all rights to the works, including the right to reproduce them in other forms. Prior to 1976, this was partly true, in that copyright to an original work of art was transferred along with title to the work in the absence of a written agreement reserving copyright to the seller. The Copyright Act of 1976 reversed this presumption. Currently, the default rule is that the people who create copyrightable works own the copyright, unless they are employees creating the work for their employers as a part of their job (independent contractors own the copyright in whatever they create, unless they assign those rights). Any transfers of copyright must be express and in writing, and this is entirely separate from any document memorializing the sale of the copyrighted work.

So although you may *own* a painting or sculpture, you may not *reproduce* its copyrighted image without the permission of the copyright owner, usually the artist. The copyright owner may, however, make reproductions in the same or other media. Armen once purchased a unique painting only to learn that the artist later made a series of serigraphs based on the painting, while Armen still had the original painting hanging in his home. Such practice of making lithographs and posters of popular works of art is common today. Only the copyright owner, or someone licensed by the copyright owner, has the right to make such reproductions. Licenses usually require paying the copyright owner a royalty based on the nature and scope of the intended use.

Some pieces may see a reduction in market value from the creation of reproductions, which is frustrating to the collector owning the original. However, this practice serves to provide the artist with a means by which to continue to profit from their work without obligating a share of future sales of the original work to the artist, as may be required in foreign countries (see chapter 7).

Non-fungible tokens (NFTs), discussed previously in this book, are unique coded registrations of digital or physical art and collectible items on the blockchain. Someone paid Beeple $69 million to acquire an NFT of his jpeg artwork entitled *Everydays: The First 5,000 Days.* But so far as we know, that person did not acquire copyright to the work. Copyright can be transferred with a physical, or digital, work, or with an NFT, but this requires an additional written document beyond any documentation of the work's sale.

As sellers brainstorm new ways to capitalize on the potential premium value placed on NFTs in the art and collectibles markets, copyright ownership becomes more crucial than ever to complete a sale. The owner of the work *Free Comb with Pagoda* by Jean-Michel Basquiat attempted a unique sale of the work. The concept was that the owner would create an NFT of the work, then destroy the actual physical work, ensuring that the NFT was the "only remaining form" of the work and therefore secure reproduction and intellectual property rights. But the owner of *Free Comb with Pagoda* did not have the copyrights they were offering for sale; those were still owned by Basquiat's estate, who quickly intervened and the offer was removed.

The problem faced by the owner of *Free Comb with Pagoda* was that they didn't own the copyrights to the work, so they couldn't sell an image of it. But video of the act of destroying a work of art is a separate creation in and of itself. A company called Injective Protocol purchased one of five hundred editions of *Morons (White)* by Banksy, which they then videotaped themselves burning and offered the video as an NFT itself.

Similarly, destroying a counterfeit does not require copyrights from the original work. Artist Cj Hendry is known for photorealistic illustrations, but when she drew an identical copy of a famous photograph of Andy Warhol and Jean-Michel Basquiat, taken by Michael Halsband, she was potentially stepping on the photographer's copyrights. Halsband defended his rights, sending a cease and desist notice and demanding that she destroy the work. And she did, but in doing so created an entirely new work. Hendry videotaped herself spray-painting the entire drawing in black and auctioned the video as an NFT titled *Copyright Infringement*, which sold for more than $37,000.

While it may seem contradictory to Congress's intentions for copyright protections, creating an NFT of the *destruction* of a work of art is not copyright infringement while creating an NFT of the work itself (whether or not the physical work is then destroyed) is infringement. Were the owner of an NFT to capture an image of the art before it is destroyed and publish that image separately (as an NFT or printed), they would be once again in the realm of copyright infringement.

Whether or not a particular work of art is protected by copyright is beyond the scope of this book, although if it carries a copyright notice—the © symbol followed by the artist's name and the date of publication—chances are it was protected by copyright at some point. But the converse is not true—items that do not bear a copyright notice may still be copyrighted. Do not be fooled by a museum's use of artwork on brochures or gift shop items such as T-shirts, mugs, and notepads. In some cases, the works being reproduced may be in the public domain, but museums also obtain permission from artists or their estates for reproducing their works. Moreover, nonprofit educational institutions have greater rights to use copyrighted images than do commercial enterprises.

So if you purchase a painting from the artist, unless you have a written agreement saying the artist assigns you the copyrights to the painting, all you have purchased is that actual physical painting. The artist has retained the copyrights. And while you can resell the painting whenever you want, you cannot make copies of the painting to sell.

Collectibles, on the other hand, rarely carry any copyrights. If Babe Ruth signs a baseball he doesn't have a copyright interest in the ball; nor does an author have a copyright interest in a rare first edition copy of their works. However, a photograph of that baseball or book is copyrighted by the photographer (or company the photographer works for), as may be the description of the item.

How long do copyright protections last? If the work was:

Published before 1923	The work is in the public domain; no copyright protections.
Published between 1923 and 1978	The work is under copyright protection for ninety-five years from the date it was published.
Not published but registered with the copyright office before 1978	The work is under copyright protection for twenty-eight years from the date of registration, with the option to renew for another sixty-seven years.
Published from 1978 to the present	The work is under copyright protection for the entirety of the creator's life plus seventy years after his or her death. If more than one person is credited for creating the work, the copyright runs through the last surviving person.

The rule of thumb we apply is, if a client wants to reproduce a work that was published less than ninety-five years ago, the client should have us research its copyright history.

An additional caveat to copyright ownership pertains to works created by the US government. The United States *can* own copyrights that originally belonged to a private citizen who then transferred the rights to the government. For example, an artist can transfer his or her copyrights to the government, or an independent contractor hired by the government may assign its copyright to the government. In those situations, the copyright exists and is held by the US government. However, if the

US government, through its employees, creates something that would normally be entitled to copyright protection, the United States does not receive those copyrights, they are immediately in the public domain.

This caveat of works created by the government is most frequently found in terms of numismatics and philately (the collection of coins or currency and stamps, respectively). While in theory the design of a coin or stamp may be entitled to copyright protection, if the design was created by a US employee, they are in the public domain.

Consult a copyright attorney if you want to reproduce works of art for commercial purposes. Copyright is the most important property right artists have, and artists are quite vigilant in enforcing their legal rights.

FAIR USE ISSUES WITH DISPLAYING ARTWORK AND DATA

Whether you're sharing the most recent addition to your collection with your social media followers, or advertising an item you are offering for sale, you want to be sure that the photographs and descriptions of the item you use are in compliance with copyright laws. We all want to be law abiding, but an extra incentive here is that the monetary penalties for violating copyrights can be steep. The owner of a copyright can always choose to ask for the actual monetary loss they've suffered by infringement. For example, if you buy a painting or comic book and then sell copies of the painting or comic book cover on posters or mugs through Etsy, the original artist could bring a copyright infringement lawsuit.

In such a lawsuit, the artist would have the option of actual or statutory damages, either of which may be costly, and may even leave you footing the bill for both yours and your opponent's attorneys' fees! Actual damages are the monetary amount the artist may have lost. Here, for example, the artist would argue that every poster or mug you sold would have been sold by him and he may win a court order divesting you of all your profits.

Statutory damages range from $200 to $150,000 per infringement. In this example, each poster and mug sold would be a new infringement. Where you fall on the range of statutory damages is based primarily on how willful your infringement was, though courts also take into account how much money you made and how much it hurt the artist's business and goodwill. Ultimately, however, even if you were innocent, had no knowledge that you didn't own the copyrights to that Spiderman #1 cover, it might still cost you two hundred dollars and attorneys' fees for each twenty-dollar mug you sold online.

The penalties don't stop there when it comes to copyrighted work on the Internet or other electronic copies. The Digital Millennium Copyright Act (known as the DMCA) aims to provide additional protections to copyrighted work that is available online or electronically, owing to the ease with which a copyrighted work online may be copied. The DMCA has three main parts: (1) copyright management information (CMI), (2) electronic copyright protections, and (3) takedown notice procedures.

Copyright management information (CMI) is any type of notice about who the copyright owner is, and the DMCA prohibits removing or manipulating CMI. For example, if you view an item listed for auction on the Heritage Auctions website, under the image of the item you will see "Imaged by Heritage Auctions, HA.com." If you buy the item and post that image on your Instagram, but crop out that text, you have removed the CMI and violated the DMCA. Even cropping out the "Imaged by" portion of the line so it simply reads "Heritage Auctions, HA.com" may be viewed as violating the DMCA because someone might read that to mean you bought the item from Heritage, not that Heritage took that photograph. Violating the DMCA by removing or altering CMI carries statutory damages of $2,500 to $25,000.

Electronic copyright protections are electronic safeguards to prevent copying. A common example is software on a DVD that prevents you from copying the movie. The DMCA prohibits either circumventing such safeguards yourself or providing the means to do so to anyone else. While lifting code off of a DVD may sound like a concern limited to professional hackers and pirates, it actually includes simpler means of circumvention. For example, if you create an account and login to the *New York Times* to view their articles, but then your account is suspended so you create a new account in another name, you've circumvented the New York Times' protections. Violating the DMCA by circumventing copyright protections carries statutory damages of $200 to $2,500 per act of circumvention (which counts as a separate circumvention each time you login under the secondary account, each copy of the DVD you make, etc.).

Finally, the DMCA provides a procedure for how to notify websites of copyright infringement on their websites. This procedure has benefits for both the websites and the copyright owners. A website that allows users to post content on their website (like eBay) would be overburdened if it were required to vet all content for potential copyright infringement and be held liable for the infringement that it missed. So instead, the website can gain "safe harbor" status by registering with the US Copyright Office under the DMCA, and setting up a simple and direct way for copyright owners to contact the website and notify them if there is an infringement issue. For example, a photographer takes a picture of Stan Lee holding a comic book that he just autographed, and now the owner of that autographed comic book is selling it on eBay and they use the photograph of Stan Lee holding the comic book. The photographer owns the copyright to that specific photograph and did not give permission (or receive a license fee) to the seller to use the photo. The photographer can go to the DMCA Agent Directory at https://www.copyright.gov/dmca-directory/ and then send a "take down notice" to the eBay DMCA Agent. eBay then has the chance to take down the photo without suffering any penalties. The safe harbor only protects eBay; the photographer could still pursue the seller for copyright infringement, though the fees will likely be reduced because the photograph was taken down.

So how do you publish images or descriptions of an item you own without running afoul of the copyrights belonging to the artist that created the work, the photographer (or their employer) who took images available online of the item, and the author (or their employer) who wrote a description of the item for an online sale or article? "Fair use" allows for certain types of copyright infringement that are generally considered to promote the goals of copyright law (promoting science and the arts, including through the creation of new information, aesthetics, insights, understandings, etc.) without stepping on the toes of existing copyrights.

Why are you posting the image or description? If you won an item at an online auction and want to share the good news with your friends and family via social media before the item is even shipped to you, using a photo from the auction house website is likely to fall under fair use as long as you credit the source of the photo. However, if you stand to profit financially from the post—whether that's because you're listing the item for sale online or you profit from subscriptions or ads on your social media—the fair use defense is unlikely to protect you. You're safer taking your own photograph of the item.

Also, remember to check the terms and conditions of the auction website you purchased from, they likely specifically state what you can and cannot do with any images you find on their website and you may have agreed to those terms and conditions when you created your account to participate in the auction.

POSTING IMAGES OF COPYRIGHTED ITEMS THAT ARE FOR SALE: THE "FIRST SALE RULE"

What if the item itself is copyrighted? If you bought a comic book originally published in 1980, it will still be covered by copyright protections that you don't own simply because you own a copy of the comic book. If you take a photograph of the cover and sell copies of that photograph, that would be infringing the rights of the original comic artist, but if you take a photograph to post online in connection with selling the one copy you own, that is acceptable because it is necessary to identify the comic book you are selling and to show potential buyers the condition of your specimen.

The United States applies what is called the "first sale doctrine" to sales of copyrighted works by persons other than the work's author. This doctrine, which is codified by federal statute at 17 U.S.C. § 109(a), provides that

> [T]he owner of a particular copy . . . lawfully made under this title, or any person authorized by such owner, is entitled, without the authority of the copyright owner, to sell or otherwise dispose of the possession of that copy. . . .[1]

The statute further extends this sale right to include the right to display an image of the work:

> [T]he owner of a particular copy lawfully made under this title, or any person authorized by such owner, is entitled, without the authority of the copyright owner, to display that copy publicly.[2]

---

[1] 17 U.S.C. § 109(a).

[2] *Id.* § 109(c).

The US Copyright Office recognizes:

> [T]he first sale doctrine, codified in 17 U.S.C. § 109, generally permits the lawful owner of a copyrighted work "to sell or otherwise dispose of the possession of that copy" and to "display that copy publicly" without the authorization of the creator.[3]

The first sale doctrine has been part of US law since at least 1908, when the US Supreme Court declared invalid a book publisher's restriction on resales of its books on copyright infringement grounds. The Supreme Court's most recent exposition of the doctrine was in *Kirtsaeng v. John Wiley & Sons, Inc.*,[4] a case involving the importation into the United States of foreign-made books against restrictions imposed by the publishers who were trying to protect their US markets against cheaper foreign-printed copies of the same works. The Court referenced a "friend of the court" brief from the Association of Art Museum Directors as to how any weakening of the first sale doctrine would affect their ability to display works by twentieth- and twenty-first-century artists that might still be subject to copyright. The Court noted that "reliance on the 'first sale' doctrine is deeply imbedded in the practices of those, such as book sellers, libraries, museums, and retailers, who have long relied upon its protection," and that it rejected "the absurd result that the copyright owner can exercise downstream control even when it authorized the import or first sale."

A leading case is *Rosen v. eBay*,[5] which involved a photographer's attempt to prevent eBay from displaying images of copyrighted photographs that an eBay seller had listed for sale. The court noted that "eBay's use of the images is to provide information to legitimate purchasers under the first sale doctrine, not for the artistic purpose of Rosen's original images," and that "eBay is not using Rosen's work to compete with Rosen . . . [T]here is nonetheless an important public benefit in allowing a thriving second-hand market for copyrighted material, and especially visual copyrighted material." This decision was, in turn, relied upon by a different federal judge in New York to dismiss a

---

3 https://www.copyright.gov/docs/resaleroyalty/.

4 Kirtsaeng v. John Wiley & Sons, Inc., 568 U.S. 519 (2013).

5 Rosen v. eBay, 2015 WL 1600081 (C.D.Cal. Jan. 16, 2015).

photographer's lawsuit against the owner of original photographs who was offering them online with accompanying images.[6]

OTHER CONSIDERATIONS

Is the photo accurate? Another reason to not use someone else's old photograph of an item in your collection is that the photo may no longer be accurate, causing the buyer of that item to return it.

Descriptions can be copyrighted works too! The way someone describes an item—but not the facts about the item—can be an original creation carrying copyright protections. So while you can look to descriptions from prior auction listings of your item for factual details—who owned the item during which years—you should describe those facts in your own words. And, like with photographs of the item, you should be sure that the description is accurate as to your specific item.

Once you take your own photo of the items in your collection, or write a description, you have your own copyrighted works to protect. If you're using those photographs and descriptions for ongoing purposes and worry about infringement, consider filing a registration with the copyright office within three months of publishing the photo or description to secure your right to statutory damages and attorneys' fees if you ever need to bring a lawsuit.

In order to protect your copyrights, registered or not, it is important to know the terms and conditions of the websites you share them on. Social media sites such as Facebook, Instagram, and Twitter all carry terms and conditions that include sublicensing your copyrights.

Instagram's sublicense condition was recently tested in New York, in the case of *Sinclair v. Ziff Davis.* Sinclair, a photographer, posted a photograph of her work on her public Instagram account. Mashable, a Ziff Davis subsidiary, published an online article in which they embedded Sinclair's Instagram post to display her photograph in their article. Sinclair sued for copyright infringement and the court upheld the Instagram terms and conditions, ruling that anyone who posts on Instagram under the public setting has agreed to allow Instagram to sublicense the post to whoever Instagram chooses.

---

[6] Stern v. Lavender, 319 F. Supp. 3d 650 (S.D.N.Y. 2018).

SUMMARY

Copyright considerations for art and collectibles include the following:

- For any works created after 1922, copyright protections may still apply; everything created before 1923 is in the public domain.
- Copyrights are not transferred when a work of art is sold (copyrights must be contracted for in writing).
- Copyrights include the right to make reproductions of a work (including posting images of the work online) and remain with the artist even after they sell the original work.
- Owners of an item are allowed to publish (in print or online) images of a work they own if they are offering the item for sale, under the first sale doctrine.
- NFTs of an existing work of art are considered a reproduction of the work and therefore copyright infringement.
- However, an NFT that incorporates an existing work, such as a video destroying the existing work, may be considered its own work and contain its own copyrights (but still not the copyrights of the earlier work).
- Artists who share images of their own work online may assign limited copyrights to the social media site through which the image was posted—read those terms and conditions!

12

Telemarketing

Sales of consumer products by telephone solicitation is common, perhaps too common for some. Whether initiated with an unsolicited "cold" call, or by the customer who provides a telephone number in response to an advertisement by the seller, telemarketing has become a major channel for art and collectibles sellers, particularly those selling rare coins and precious metals. Special rules apply here, mostly requiring disclosures from the sellers to ensure that customers are informed fully about what they are getting, but also to protect consumers from abuses. Those rules apply to online sales to the extent that a telephone communication is involved.

Art and collectibles are often marketed over the telephone or on television. Often, telemarketing campaigns are intended for investors, although there are major retailers and cable television shopping networks who sell to collectors. When buying over the telephone some of the risks we've been discussing in this book may be greater, because you don't actually see the item in person before you buy, and telephone salespeople can be quite deceptive regarding quality, pricing, and liquidity. However, special protective rules and regulations apply to telephone sales as a result of recent action by Congress and the Federal Trade Commission (FTC).

In addition to the federal law and FTC regulations, dozens of states regulate telemarketing as a matter of state law. Some states merely require telemarketers to register with a state agency and pay an annual fee. Others provide for maintenance of "Do-Not-Call" lists and provide that telemarketers refrain from any calls to persons on such lists.

WHO IS A TELEMARKETER?

On January 1, 1996, the Telemarketing and Consumer Fraud and Abuse Prevention Act, 15 U.S.C. § 6101 *et seq.*, went into effect, authorizing the FTC to issue regulations requiring telemarketers to make appropriate disclosures about the nature and price of the goods or services being sold.

So, are you a telemarketer?

The Telemarketing Act defines "telemarketing" as any plan, program, or campaign that is conducted to induce payment for goods and services by use of more than one interstate telephone call. Mail order dealers persuaded the FTC to exclude from this definition telephone calls initiated by customers responding to postcards, brochures, and advertisements. However, the Act continues to apply to sales of "investment opportunities," defined as anything offered for sale, sold, or traded based on express or implied representations about income, profit, or appreciation. In such cases, even incoming calls by customers are covered by the regulations.

Here are some examples. A firm that solicits the sale of art prints or rare coins through "cold" calls is clearly covered. However, what about the companies who advertise "limited edition" or "collectible" items such as dolls, plates, and commemorative coins and medals in the Sunday magazine sections of newspapers? Where there is a mention of how prior items in a particular series have appreciated in value over time, or any hint that demand for a particular item will increase in the future, the offer would probably be considered telemarketing. However, where only the mintage is given, or the words "limited edition" are used several times, that should not cross the line into an implied representation about income, profit, or appreciation.

While this sounds like most companies in the country, there are many exceptions. The first is that each state has an exception for a minimum number of sales, so anyone who occasionally completes a sale over the phone does not need to worry. Most states excuse anyone who completes fewer than 25 percent of their sales over the phone from registering as a telemarketer. So, if you operate a website and sell online, having a phone line to assist customers who have trouble using the website shouldn't qualify.

The remaining exceptions to registration vary by state. Many states have an exception for companies that do not engage in cold calling. Cold calling is where the company calls phone numbers of persons who are not yet customers and have not indicated they are interested in becoming customers. Think of companies that buy customer lists.

Most states also have an exception if the company limits its outgoing calls to only their existing customers. This discourages many telemarketers from cold calling, instead implementing a policy where their sales representatives must wait for inbound calls from potential customers and only place outgoing calls to existing customers.

For most states, a policy of receiving calls from potential customers is acceptable without requiring telemarketing registrations, but a few states are now eliminating that exception if the potential customer's call was prompted by an advertisement. California, one of the strictest states concerning telemarketing registration, considers phone calls *from* interested potential customers to be telemarketing if they were prompted by an advertisement.

Another common exception (though not available in California) is for catalogue sellers. If a catalogue containing images, details, and descriptions of the items offered for sale is delivered to the potential customer, before or after the first phone call, but before the sale is completed, the seller does not have to register as a telemarketer.

More than thirty states now require registration of telemarketers. Registration usually entails obtaining a surety bond, submitting copies of the sales scripts given to the persons making the phone calls (updating those submissions regularly), and submitting a form that describes the products sold and gives details about the owners, managers, and sales representatives of the company (names, addresses, criminal/bankruptcy history). There is also a filing fee (which ranges from $50 to $1,500) and many states charge additional fees for companies with more than a certain number of sales representatives.

The states all generally require the same information, the most onerous of which is keeping up to date on sales scripts and the sales representatives, if you go through many scripts and or callers.

Many of the states that require telemarketers to register have variations of these and a few other exceptions, such as if the company is required to register with the state under another law, for example, for selling investments.

And while you should check the laws for each state in which you plan to make sales over the phone, most companies who conduct more than 25 percent of their business over the phone in states like

California have little hope of finding an exception to registering as a telemarketer.

REQUIREMENTS FOR TELEMARKETERS

All sales by telemarketers are subject to certain requirements under the Telemarketing Act. First, before consummating the sale, the seller must affirmatively disclose to the buyer the number of items sold, the purchase price, and the seller's refund, exchange, and buyback policies. The dealer is not *required* to have such policies, but if it does, they must be disclosed. Second, dealers must avoid misrepresenting material facts about the items being sold. As we've seen, material misrepresentations are unlawful anyway. But through the Telemarketing Act and the Telemarketing Sales Rule, Congress and the FTC enhanced the remedies available to victims of telemarketing fraud, making the Rule a major improvement in consumer protection.

The Telephone Consumer Protection Act (TCPA) contains several limitations on telemarketers that are intended to protect consumers from a barrage of unwanted phone solicitations. One of the best-known provisions of the TCPA is the requirement for companies to honor Do Not Call Registries.

The TCPA also bans the use of autodialers, which the Supreme Court has defined as software that uses a random or sequential number generator to store or produce numbers to be called. This definition came through the Supreme Court on April 1, 2021, in *Facebook, Inc. v. Duguid, et al.*[1] But the fact is that telemarketers don't use number generators anymore; software has advanced so that "autodialers" harvest and store phone numbers to use in telemarketing without generating numbers. Therefore, the *Facebook* decision, based on a rigid reading of the current statute, has rendered the current prohibition of autodialers completely obsolete. Anyone using autodialers should expect state or federal legislatures to correct this gap in the law.

Many states also have laws, all of which are very similar to one another, including such requirements as that the sales representative must identify themself and what they're selling within the first sixty seconds of the

[1] Facebook Inc. v. Duguid et al. 592 U.S. ___ (2021).

phone call, and that the seller give all buyers at least seven days to return the purchased goods.

Still others, such as California, regulate telemarketing to a much higher degree than does the federal government. California's Telephonic Sellers Law, found at California Business and Professions Code § 17511 *et seq.*, regulates both outbound and inbound calls relating to precious metals, gemstones, coins, "or any other investment opportunity of any type whatsoever." Telemarketers who advertise potential profits to customers must provide the state with data demonstrating that 50 percent of prior customers earned comparable profits, and all telemarketers must put up a $100,000 bond to satisfy consumer claims and provide customers with past performance data before any sales.

Registration and compliance with telemarketing rules may appear daunting at first, but once implemented they become easier to maintain. However, when states mandate compliance with these laws as a precondition of doing business, one might argue that any noncompliant dealers' sales are unlawful and subject to rescission at any time, though there are no cases directly on this point. The penalties for noncompliance may be far more damaging to a seller than the cost of compliance.

All of this gives consumers substantial rights, and anyone buying from a telemarketer should understand what disclosures they should be receiving, as well as what remedies are available to them in the event of problems.

SUMMARY

Before you sell art or collectibles over the telephone, consider if you are a telemarketer who needs to register.

- Are you calling potential customers (i.e., people who have not already bought items from you)?
- Are you selling art or collectibles as an investment opportunity? Are you selling precious metals?
- Do more than 25 percent of your sales occur over the telephone?
- Do you also send customers a printed catalogue with detailed descriptions of the items for sale?

Consumers should understand their rights when buying from telemarketers.

13

Additional Rights and Risks When Buying or Selling Remotely

This chapter discusses certain aspects of buying art and collectibles that are unique or especially important when buying or selling online or through the mail.

RISK OF LOSS WHEN BUYING REMOTELY

Whether buying online retail or at auction, many art and collectibles are received by mail or courier shipment from their source. Ordinarily, sellers require payment in full before shipping, and therefore the buyer must be concerned about receiving items intact and unharmed in transit. Risk of loss during shipment may be allocated between buyer and seller, and before making a mail order or auction purchase, buyers should know where the risk lies in the particular transaction. Most dealers and auction houses are insured for losses occurring during shipment to or from their places of business, and it is common for them to accept the risk of loss. Additionally, some websites facilitating sales between persons on the site, such as eBay, provide their own money-back guarantee if the seller fails to deliver the purchased item as described.

However, it is not necessarily the case that a dealer or auctioneer's insurance will pay the full retail price of an item lost, stolen, or damaged during shipment. Some insurance policies cover only fair market value, or even 80 percent of fair market value. Unless a policy expressly defines fair market value to include retail price, the insurer's payment may be based only on the item's *wholesale* value, which is substantially less than most retail buyers pay. Moreover, where items are damaged and may be subject to restoration, the insurer may pay only the restoration costs. In these situations, collectors are legitimately concerned about whether restoration adequately restores an item's pre-damage value, or whether the item should be declared a total loss.

Of course, reputable dealers will often make up any difference between the insurance proceeds and the purchase price, but many purchase invoices do not commit the dealer to do this, or expressly limit loss recoveries to actual insurance proceeds paid. With online purchases, these details may be buried in the terms and conditions. While you can always enforce the terms and conditions on the website against the seller if a problem arises, regardless of whether you read or agreed to them before the sale, it's worth reading them before you complete your purchase. Where items of substantial value are involved, if the standard terms the dealer is offering are not sufficient, it is worth asking the dealer about risk of loss and insurance and getting a copy of the dealer's insurance policy.

RETURN PRIVILEGES

Most art and collectibles dealers will permit a customer to change his or her mind about a purchase within a reasonable time and will accept return of the item(s) for a full refund with no questions asked. Some dealers, however, condition returns on authenticity problems, and some do not accept returns for any reason. Return periods are usually measured from the date the buyer receives delivery and should allow enough time to get a second opinion on the item (i.e., three business days). However, be sure to understand the terms and conditions that apply to returns. For example, with rare coins, dealers may require that the coins be returned in their original packaging. For a fine art sale, the costs of return shipping and insurance might be substantial, so make sure you understand who is responsible for those. The Telemarketing Act requires mail order dealers to disclose their return policies, but it does not require them to allow returns (only to disclose whether they do or not).

Nobody buys art or collectibles with the intent to return them. But it is prudent to know the dealer's return policy before making a purchase. Again, reviewing those terms and conditions for return policies prior to a sale may allow you time to negotiate. At a minimum, you will know if you only have a few days after receiving the item to return it so you don't let a box with a damaged item sit unopened in a corner until it's too late to return it.

SALES AND USE TAX

As will be discussed in chapter 18, the application of sales and use tax laws to art and collectibles transactions is evolving and controversial. This is not because there is anything particularly different about art and collectible items that entitles them to special treatment. Indeed, the treatment of art and collectibles for sales and use tax purposes has changed only because of changes directed at the far more significant online businesses that deliver everything from cat food to cars at the click of a mouse. In the past ten years or so, US states have attacked the legal doctrines used to shield online transactions from state and local taxes, with considerable success.

Until 2018, the long-standing rule was that a seller was only required to collect taxes for transactions in states where the seller had a physical, "brick-and-mortar" location. This was an especially useful distinction for art and collectibles dealers who bought and sold at trade shows around the country.

But as Internet sales skyrocketed, states began to see a decrease in sales taxes and more and more purchases were instead subject to use taxes. Use tax is owed by individual buyers who must report that they've made purchases out of state and therefore is far more difficult and costly for a state to trace and collect. Some online retailers, many of whom were selling to persons in all fifty states, even advertised that they did not collect taxes, implying that the purchase was tax-free unless the buyer chose to report the purchase. The states pushed back, implementing laws that streamline the states' work by requiring the out-of-state sellers to collect and report use taxes on behalf of the buyers if they had sales in excess of a threshold amount, regardless of where—or if—they had a physical location.

In 2018, the Supreme Court sided with those states in *South Dakota v. Wayfair, et al.* Under *Wayfair*,[1] all sellers with a physical location in a state, *and* any out-of-state seller who meets the state's threshold, have to report taxes. There are now more than thirty states that have relied on *Wayfair* and set a threshold and require out-of-state sellers to report taxes.

Now, whether sellers must require payment of sales or use tax on a sale of art or collectible items depends on both where the seller has a physical location and the level of business those sellers conduct in the buyer's state. There is no more anonymity for art and collectible dealers on the Internet, and taxing authorities will make themselves aware of sellers doing business with their residents. The easy case is where the seller and buyer are located in the same state. If that state imposes a sales or use tax on the items being sold, the seller must charge tax.

In the more likely situation of the seller and buyer being located in different states, the minimum threshold of business that triggers the requirement to collect sales tax varies by state, but generally the threshold is at least one hundred thousand dollars in transactions or two hundred transactions. Failure to collect sales tax from customers may result in the seller having to pay the state what it should have collected from its customers out of its own pocket instead. The famous South Dakota statute reads:

> [A]ny seller selling tangible personal property, products transferred electronically, or services for delivery into South Dakota, who does not have a physical presence in the state . . . shall remit the sales tax and shall follow all applicable procedures and requirements of law as if the seller had a physical presence in the state, provided the seller meets either of the following criteria in the previous calendar year or the current calendar year:
>
> **1.** The seller's gross revenue from the sale of tangible personal property, any product transferred electronically, or services delivered into South Dakota exceeds one hundred thousand dollars; or
>
> **2.** The seller sold tangible personal property, any product transferred electronically, or services for delivery into South Dakota in two hundred or more separate transactions.[2]

---

[1] South Dakota v. Wayfair, Inc., 585 U.S. ___ (2018).

[2] South Dakota Codified Law § 10-64-2.

Note that this statute is not limited to online sellers, but also includes telemarketers and anyone who sold into South Dakota. So both of the following situations may result in a dealer being subject to the new tax statute (as long as they meet the one hundred thousand dollars or two hundred transactions threshold): an art or collectibles dealer who physically traveled to South Dakota and completed a sale (but without establishing a brick-and-mortar storefront), or a dealer who begins a transaction at a trade show that is then completed by email with a buyer from South Dakota.

Given that art and collectible items are frequently very high-priced, the one-hundred-thousand-dollar threshold is met by nearly all significant dealers in nearly all states. So online customers should expect to pay sales or use tax on their purchases.

THE AMERICANS WITH DISABILITIES ACT

The Americans with Disabilities Act (ADA) requires that "places of public accommodation" offer disabled persons equal access to the goods and services offered. The ADA is generally thought of as applying to physical stores, hotels, restaurants, and so on. Our first thoughts are ramps and wheelchair-accessible restrooms. Dealers of art and collectibles are not insensitive to the needs of collectors with disabilities, but rarely will concern themselves with the ADA because they either rent a space open to the public which is already ADA compliant, or they only operate wholesale, remotely, or through visiting other person's locations, like trade shows and auctions.

But does the ADA apply to your website? Websites usually face accessibility issues in relation to enabling screen-reading software for blind persons, but implementing the code necessary to facilitate screen-reading software can be onerous (especially in comparison to offering a phone number that persons unable to use the website can call to receive assistance in completing a transaction).

The question is not entirely settled. Several federal circuit courts have issued rulings that some or all websites are exempt from ADA compliance.[3] In April 2021, the Eleventh Circuit overturned a Florida

[3] Biden v. Knight First Amendment Inst. Etc., 593 U.S. __ (2021)(Thomas, J., concurring).

District Court ruling in *Gil v. Winn-Dixie Stores, Inc.*[4] The district court had ruled that because the Winn-Dixie grocery stores were covered by the ADA, the website that provided services in relation to the stores, such as ordering a prescription refill that the customer picks up at a store in person, must also be compliant under the ADA.[5] The Eleventh Circuit reviewed the ADA and came to the conclusion that only physical locations are subject to the ADA requirements. The Third and Sixth Circuits have similarly held since the 1990s that websites are not places of public accommodation under the ADA.[6]

The Ninth Circuit has taken a position more similar to the Florida District Court in *Winn-Dixie* before the Eleventh Circuit's reversal. The Ninth Circuit has ruled that while a website is not a place of public accommodation itself, if the website is a service of a company that has physical locations and is a place of public accommodation, the website needs to be ADA compliant.[7] Since 2015, the Ninth Circuit has dismissed ADA lawsuits against eBay and Netflix because their "services are not connected to any actual, physical place," but did apply the ADA to the Domino's Pizza website and phone app because they "connect customers to the goods and services of Domino's physical restaurants."[8]

No other federal circuit court has ruled directly on this issue, though the First and Seventh Circuits have shown an inclination to at least follow in the Ninth Circuit's footsteps of subjecting some websites to the ADA's requirements. Both the First and Seventh Circuits have reviewed cases where a plaintiff sought to apply the ADA's requirements to insurance policies on the grounds that insurance offices are places of

---

[4] Gil v. Winn-Dixie Stores, Inc., Case No. 17-13467 (11th Cir. Apr. 7, 2021).

[5] Gil v. Winn Dixie Stores, Inc., 242 F. Supp. 3d 1315 (S.D. FL 2017).

[6] Ford v. Schering-Plough Corp., 145 F.3d 601 (3d Cir. 1998); Peoples v. Discover Fin. Servs., Inc., 387 F. App'x 179 (3d Cir. 2010); Parker v. Metro. Life Ins. Co., 121 F.3d 1006 (6th Cir. 1997).

[7] Weyer v. Twentieth Century Fox Film Corp., 198 F.3d 1104 (9th Cir. 2000).

[8] Cullen v. Netflix, Inc. No. 13-14092 (9th Cir. Mar. 13, 2015); Earll v. eBay, Inc., No. 13-151334 (9th Cir. Mar. 13, 2015); and Robles v. Domino's Pizza, LLC, 913 F.3d 898 (2019).

public accommodation.[9] Both circuits ruled that the ADA was not limited to physical locations in applying the ADA to the services offered at those insurance offices and even indicated that "electronic places" were places of public accommodation.

The Second Circuit has issued a similar ruling on insurance policies but stopped short of indicating how it would rule on whether electronic spaces[10]—that is, websites—could be places of public accommodation.

SUMMARY

Additional considerations when buying and selling remotely include the following:

- Know how much insurance (and the seller) will pay for items lost or damaged during shipment (which usually occurs after payment).
- Know your return privileges and be diligent in obtaining any second opinion as to authenticity, condition, and value within that time.
- Know that the seller is likely obligated to collect taxes on remote sales if their total sales into that state exceed one hundred thousand dollars (even if through multiple transactions).
- Know that the law is still evolving as to whether a seller's website must be ADA compliant even if it is entirely remote.

---

[9] Carparts Distri. Ctr. v. Automotive Wholesaler's Ass'n., 37 F.3d 12 (1st Cir. 1994); and Doe v. Mutual of Omaha Ins. Co., 179 F.3d 557 (7th Cir. 1999).

[10] Pallozzi v. Allstate Life Ins. Co., 198 F.3d 28 (2d Cir. 1999).

PART 4
Additional Considerations Unique to Certain Art and Collectibles

Certain art and collectibles carry additional rules or complications that a buyer or seller should be aware of before entering into a transaction. This part of the book discusses art and collectibles that may be illegal in certain circumstances, such as government property that was not authorized to be owned privately, or when importing items that are designated as stolen cultural property by a foreign country.

14

Illegal Art or Collectibles

Believe it or not, some art and collectible items are illegal to own, or restricted in their importation and sale.

ILLEGAL UNITED STATES COINS AND GOVERNMENT PROPERTY

Today, certain US coins are actually illegal to own in the United States.

A great example of this captivated coin collectors for twenty years as it played out in federal courts in New York City and Philadelphia. A British rare coin dealer was arrested in a sting operation for trying to sell an undercover Secret Service agent a US 1933 twenty-dollar gold piece. These aren't ordinary collectible US coins. In March 1933, as part of his efforts to stabilize the US economy after taking office, President Franklin Roosevelt eliminated the use of gold coins as currency and outlawed private ownership of gold except for "rare and unusual coins" held by collectors.[1] The 1933 twenty-dollar gold pieces that had already been minted were never issued, and subsequently were melted down. However, prior to Roosevelt's order, apparently a few examples of the coin had left the mint in an unknown way.

Even though the ban on gold ownership has long since been repealed, the government's position ever since 1933 has been that those coins are subject to confiscation without compensation. Needless to say, the coin

---

[1] Executive Order 6102. Repealed by Pub. L. 93–373 (December 31, 1974).

is quite rare today, although not "rare and unusual" by 1933's standards. Many numismatic scholars say that examples of the coin left quite legally when individuals approached mint personnel and traded in older twenty-dollar gold pieces on a one-to-one basis, and they are appalled that the government could make it illegal to own a US legal tender coin.

The charges against the British dealer were dropped, and ultimately it turned out that his coin had once been owned by King Farouk of Egypt, an avid coin collector, who acquired the coin in the United States and successfully obtained an export permit for it from the US Department of the Treasury—the same agency that was supposed to enforce the gold coin prohibitions—in the 1940s. Fearing losing its civil case and having to return the coin to the dealer, the government agreed to "monetize" it and sell it at auction, splitting the proceeds equally with the British dealer. The coin sold for $7.59 million in July 2002 to an anonymous buyer, who was recently revealed to have been the shoe designer Stuart Weitzman. Weitzman sold the coin in June 2021 for $18.87 million. The owners of ten other specimens of this coin fared less well, losing their rights after federal court proceedings in Philadelphia determined that the coins probably were removed from government premises unlawfully.[2]

CURRENCY REPLICAS

Among other "illegal" artworks are those that too closely resemble US currency (the talented artist J.S.G. Boggs has made a career out of painting reproductions of US paper money and feuding with the Secret Service over his First Amendment right to do so), or contain images classified as "child pornography" under state statutes. In 1989, general obscenity laws resulted in the closing of critically acclaimed exhibitions by photographer Robert Mapplethorpe. And each year Congress considers legislation to ban artwork that desecrates the US flag or subjects it to ridicule. A constitutional amendment may eventually be passed to protect the flag. The pros and cons of art and the First Amendment are a book in themselves.

Some types of collectibles also are illegal to sell. A federal law entitled the Hobby Protection Act prohibits the sale of replica coins or

[2] Langbord v. U.S. Dept. of the Treasury, 888 F.Supp.2d 606 (2012) *cert. denied*, 137 S.Ct. 1578 (2017).

political memorabilia unless the word "COPY" is conspicuously placed on one side of the item.[3] Regulations prescribe the size and location of the COPY notice, and it is practically impossible to mistake a properly marked replica item for the genuine article (which, of course, is the purpose of the Act). Congress feared the proliferation of collectibles in the 1970s would encourage counterfeiters, and the Hobby Protection Act provides some limited protection. Replicas of collectible items may also be restricted by federal trademark and unfair competition statutes, most notably the Lanham Act and equivalent state laws.[4]

SUMMARY

Before buying or selling art and collectibles, ensure that it is legal to own in the United States.

- Certain US gold coins are illegal to own, specifically the 1933 twenty-dollar gold pieces (other than the specimen once owned by King Farouk of Egypt).
- Imitations of coins and paper currency that too closely resemble US currency may be illegal, unless they conspicuously state "COPY."
- Some states maintain obscenity laws that classify certain artistic images as "child pornography," and general obscenity laws have been used against works depicting homosexuality.
- Art depicting the US flag in a disparaging light is regularly under threat of congressional action, but as of the time of writing, no law has been passed.

---

3 15 U.S.C. §§ 2101–2106.

4 15 U.S.C. § 1125(a).

15

Buying and Importing Cultural Property

This is an increasingly difficult area of the art law field, and is so intertwined with politics, religion, and national attitudes that whole books have been devoted to it. This book will focus on the problems that may be associated with purchasing certain types of art, antiquities, and collectibles that have been specially classified under international treaties or US federal and state laws.

Many of the world's most famous collections of ancient art and artifacts were acquired by theft, during periods when European countries controlled areas beyond their own borders, such as Greece, Egypt, and the Far East. A famous example of this are the so-called "Elgin Marbles," a group of marble sculptures from the Acropolis in Athens that were removed and taken to Great Britain in the early 1800s and are on display at the British Museum in London. Lord Elgin claimed to have received permission from the Sultan of the Ottoman Empire to cut and remove these objects, but this is hotly contested today, and even at the time the poet Lord Byron condemned the removals as vandalism.[1] A more recent example comes from the 1990s, when an exhibition of Trojan gold jewelry and artifacts opened in Moscow. These treasures were excavated in Turkey by Heinrich Schliemann, the great German archeologist credited with discovering the site of ancient Troy. Schliemann bequeathed

[1] Lord Byron, "The Curse of Minerva." 1807.

the items to the German government, but in 1945, in the aftermath of World War II, Russian soldiers removed them from a Nazi hiding place and took them to Russia. The governments of Turkey, Germany, and Russia all have declared that the items are their "cultural property." And even in the United States, nobody disputes that a huge amount of Native American material has been excavated and removed without knowledge or consent of the peoples involved. And so on throughout the world.

The growing influence of formerly colonized nations, combined with feelings of guilt among former colonialist nations that happen to be major consumers of art and collectibles, has led to certain international and domestic legislation regulating the trade in what is called "cultural property." Anyone interested in buying antiquities or items of obvious historic, cultural, or religious significance should understand certain basic principles. First, what is cultural property? The term is defined in compromise fashion in some of the federal laws on the subject. The Customs Service's definition includes (1) objects of "archeological interest" at least 250 years old; (2) objects of "ethnological interest" that originated with "tribal or non-industrial" societies and are "important to the cultural heritage of a people"; (3) a catchall category of "cultural property" including property "relating to history," pieces of historic monuments, antiquities and coins more than one hundred years old, postage stamps, furniture items more than one hundred years old, rare books and manuscripts, and original paintings, sculptures, engravings, and prints.[2]

Second, is it legal to own cultural property? Sometimes. Beyond that truism, however, there are some signs buyers should look for to avoid the risk of having their purchases taken from them. While it is legal to own certain items, it might not be legal to import them. In 1983, the United States enacted the Convention on Cultural Property Implementation Act,[3] which implemented into US law the 1970 UNESCO Convention on the Means of Prohibiting and Preventing the Illicit Import, and Export, and Transfer of Ownership of Cultural Property. This law, usually referred to as the CPIA, joined the United States in an international effort to restrict importation of items that other countries have declared to be illicitly obtained cultural property. Traditionally, the United States

---

[2] 19 CFR 12.104.

[3] 19 U.S.C. § 2601.

did not honor the laws of other countries in this area, and for that reason art dealers, collectors, and museums were able to acquire and import works that could not legally have been exported from their countries of origin. Ironically, the ardent opposition of art dealers to enactment of the UNESCO Convention into US law was overcome only by the realization that many US Customs officials were (over) zealously stopping items of cultural property on the authority of the National Stolen Property Act, and that the Convention might restrict those officers to seizing only specified categories of goods.

The CPIA authorizes import restrictions on archaeological objects "first discovered within" and "subject to export control by" a specific State Party to the 1970 UNESCO Convention that are illicitly exported from that same State Party after the effective date of implementing regulations.[4] Congress granted US Customs and Border Protection (CBP) broad discretion to detain artifacts on "designated lists" for investigation, while giving importers the right to contest seizures in court, under procedures requiring the government to prove by expert testimony or other admissible evidence that the objects were illicitly exported from the State Party after the effective date of the regulations.[5]

Following the CPIA's enactment, a group of ancient coin dealers imported certain Cypriot and Chinese coins into the United States without identifying their "find spots," in order to precipitate a test case. The coins were seized and forfeited by the US government, and the dealers went to court to seek their return. This eventually resulted in a 2018 Fourth Circuit decision focused on the uncontested fact that the coins were of types found on "designated lists" negotiated between the US State Department and the governments of Cyprus and China in 2007 and 2009, respectively, under the UNESCO Convention rubric.[6] The Fourth Circuit had earlier approved the seizure of these same coins without considering the coins' possible forfeiture.[7] In this second appeal, the court applied its earlier dicta as binding precedent, but examined

---

[4] 19 U.S.C. §§ 2601, 2604, 2606.

[5] 19 U.S.C. §§ 2606, 2610.

[6] U.S. v. Ancient Coin Collectors Guild, 899 F.3d 295 (4th Cir. 2018).

[7] Ancient Coin Collectors Guild v. U.S. Customs and Border Protection, 698 F.3d 171 (4th Cir. 2012).

the bases for it anyway. We represented three coin dealer and collector organizations as "friends of the court" in both appeals.

The court emphasized the process by which the "designated lists" of items subject to seizure and forfeiture are created. In particular, the court noted that Congress created a Cultural Property Advisory Committee (CPAC) made up of a diverse group of what the court called "experts and stakeholders in 'the international exchange of archeological and ethnological materials.'"[8] In the court's view, the "designated lists" are created only after CPAC "conduct[s] an investigation and prepare[s] a report detailing whether import restrictions are warranted," the president considers that report before entering into memorandums of understanding (MOUs), and then the State Department prepares lists accordingly.[9]

The plaintiff dealers challenged whether this process was, in fact, followed with respect to the "designated lists" of coins created pursuant to the Cyprus and China MOUs. It alleged that (1) CPAC recommended against import restrictions on Cypriot coins and was not allowed to make any recommendations on Chinese coins; (2) the State Department misled the Congress and public about CPAC's true recommendations on Cypriot coins in official government reports; and (3) there was at least an appearance of conflict of interest involving "the decision-maker [who] approved import restrictions on Cypriot coins" based on her connections with a prominent campaigner for import restrictions on cultural goods. The import of all this, according to the plaintiffs, was that CBP was authorized to seize the plaintiffs' coins without any evidence that the coins were "first discovered within" and "subject to export control by" the countries to which they were being repatriated, and that Congress's extremely narrow statutory framework was being ignored. While all these same arguments had been made during the first appeal, the plaintiffs re-emphasized their importance when the due process rights of US citizens were at stake.

The Fourth Circuit's response was simple. Having conceded that the coins in the government's forfeiture complaint were on the "designated lists," and that they knew this to be the case at the time of importation, the plaintiffs could defeat forfeiture only by establishing that the coins either had been exported from Cyprus or China before the

---

8 U.S. v. Ancient Coin Collectors Guild, 899 F.3d 295 (4th Cir. 2018).

9 *Id.*

restrictions took effect, or by lawful license thereafter, citing 19 U.S.C. § 2606(c)(2)(A) and (B). The court rejected the plaintiffs' contention that the government had to prove that these particular coins were "first discovered in" or "subject to export control by" Cyprus or China, finding that those requirements applied only at the initial stage of CPAC reporting, MOUs, and creation of the lists themselves. The court cited both its earlier nonforfeiture decision and the courts' inability to "second-guess[] the executive branch's international negotiations regarding issues of cultural heritage." In evaluating the plaintiffs' due process challenges, the court noted that the government's initial burden was such that successful forfeitures would not happen without such strong evidence that the importer must have had "fair notice" that the items were on designated lists and, therefore, subject to forfeiture. The court noted that the plaintiffs did not contend that the lists themselves were insufficiently "specific and precise" to notify it that the coins they were importing would be subject to forfeiture.

Implicit in the Fourth Circuit's opinion is the fact that Congress established a certain process for creating the "designated lists" of items subject to seizure, and that this process involved diplomatic and scholarly judgments that courts are not competent to revisit in the context of litigation. In effect, the court was telling the plaintiffs to direct their "first discovery" and "subject to export control by" arguments to the CPAC and State Department in order to influence the lists themselves, rather than litigate over whether items concededly on the lists should be seized by CBP and forfeited. While superficially attractive, this view condones the usurpation of power by executive agencies beyond that given by Congress, a situation that federal courts deal with continually without complaint. It is true that the whiff of foreign policy considerations often frightens courts into accepting executive actions; in this case the Fourth Circuit was dealing with the CPIA, a US domestic statute intended to restrict the use of the CBP on behalf of foreign governments to a somewhat narrow sphere of items provably looted from those countries. This decision is a step backward in honoring Congress's intent.

The upshot of all this is that items of cultural property that were not legally exported from their country of origin cannot legally be imported into the United States. Foreign countries maintain lists of such works, as well as of works that have been reported stolen from their museums or sacred sites. Items that make it into the United States are not affected by the law. They are, however, subject to state laws requiring replevin of stolen property, as we'll see later in the case of the Cypriot mosaics.

In the 1990s, UNIDROIT, another international organization, proposed a treaty allowing private actions against "possessors" of stolen or illegally exported cultural property, which would have included museums, art restorers, and dealers or auction houses holding goods on consignment.[10] UNIDROIT's treaty, which became effective in July 1998, does not require compensation unless the possessors prove that they held the items in good faith. Although thirty-seven countries ratified the treaty, neither the United States nor most art market countries (China excepted) have ratified it, and it is not US law. The United States is highly unlikely to even adopt a treaty that essentially requires US courts to enforce other countries' definitions of both "cultural property" and "illegal export," no matter how much those definitions might differ from those in the United States.

UNIDROIT notwithstanding, when it comes to Native American art or artifacts, US federal and state laws protect sites and require identification and return of any illicitly acquired property. Three of the major laws in this area are the Pre-Columbian Monument Act,[11] the Native American Graves Protection and Repatriation Act (NAGPRA),[12] and the New Mexico Cultural Properties Act.[13] Under NAGPRA, for example, Native American sacred objects and items of cultural patrimony excavated or discovered after November 1990 must be returned to the tribal nation upon whose land they were found, or another nation with "close cultural affiliation" to the items. However, an organized tribal nation must assert rights to particular items. If they do not, collectors may keep them legally. This law, and the belief that Native American nations often don't have the capacity or the desire to maintain and preserve artifacts, has led some to challenge the entire concept of federal intervention in the art field, a controversy beyond the scope of this book.

---

[10] Institut International Pour L'Unification Du Droit Prive (UNIDROIT) (International Institute for the Unification of Private Law) Convention on Stolen or Illegally Exported Cultural Objects (Rome, 24 June, 1995).

[11] 19 U.S.C. § 2091.

[12] 25 U.S.C. § 3001 *et seq.*

[13] NMSA 18-6-1.

Even if works are not technically "cultural property" under the international treaties or federal statutes, because they were imported into the United States prior to enactment of the relevant laws, they may still be subject to common law replevin principles in the state where they are located. A good example of this is the landmark case of *Autocephalous Greek Orthodox Church v. Goldberg Feldman Arts,*[14] where an Indianapolis art dealer paid more than one million dollars to purchase Byzantine mosaics, which turned out to have been looted from a church in Cyprus in the aftermath of the civil war there in the mid-1970s. The government of Cyprus relied upon Indiana law in bringing suit in 1989 to recover its stolen personal property. The court awarded the mosaics back to Cyprus, rejecting the dealer's arguments that the government did not use due diligence and that as an innocent purchaser, return of the mosaics would be unjust:

> Lest this result seem too harsh, we should note that those who wish to purchase art work on the international market, undoubtedly a ticklish business, are not without means to protect themselves. Especially when circumstances are as suspicious as those that faced Peg Goldberg, prospective purchasers would do best to do more than make a few last-minute phone calls. As testified to at trial, in a transaction like this, "All the red flags are up, all the red lights are on, all the sirens are blaring."

One final word on cultural property for those thinking of buying art abroad. Some foreign countries restrict export not only of important works that originated there, but of *any important work present within their boundaries.* For example, until recently Argentina did not allow any works of art to leave at all. And in a celebrated case in 1995–96, the French government was required to pay dearly for its export restrictions. Apparently in 1989, France declared Van Gogh's *Jardin à Auvers* a historical monument, which could not be exported. At the time, the painting was in France, having been brought there by its owner, Swiss national Jacques Walter. Walter eventually sold the painting at auction in Paris for $10.2 million, but sued the government, claiming that the sale price was severely reduced by the export restriction. The court awarded Walter $29 million that, according to published reports, is almost two

---

[14] Autocephalous Ch. v. Goldberg Feldman Arts, 917 F.2d 278 (7th Cir. 1990).

year's budget for the Musées Nationaux in France. Such incidents have not, however, cooled countries' fervor concerning the loss of important artworks. In May 2021, the British government imposed an export ban on a late fifteenth-century bronze rondel from Mantua, Italy, valued at £17 million, despite the fact that the artist is unknown, based on its "remarkable craftsmanship, aesthetics and mystery."

SUMMARY

Restrictions on cultural property vary based on the item, its location, and whether it has been removed from its place of origin. Therefore, before buying or selling art or collectibles, know whether the item is cultural property that may be subject to restrictions.

- Is the item of archeological, ethnological, or historical interest?
- What is the provenance of the item and how was it discovered?
- In what country was it created? And, if an archeological item, in what country was it excavated/rediscovered?
- When was it excavated/rediscovered?

Get as much provenance information as possible in writing before making a purchase and keep that information should a claim arise later.

PART 5
Dispute Resolution in Art and Collectibles Transactions

As with transactions for goods or services of any kind, disputes unfortunately arise. However, the unique aspects of art and collectibles can add complications, such as where an item is not discovered to be inauthentic until the buyer attempts to resell the item thirty years after purchase. Congress has recently directed the US Copyright Office to create a new dispute resolution process similar to a small-claims court. And the uniqueness of art and collectibles means that in many disputes the parties are fighting over the physical item itself rather than monetary damages.

16

Negotiation, Arbitration, and Litigation

Our experience has been that most art and collectibles dealers and auctioneers want satisfied customers and will try to resolve problems promptly. This chapter explains some methods for dispute resolution that are used in this area, and where to go if all else fails.

NEGOTIATION: WORKING IT OUT WITH THE DEALER

If you think you have a problem with an art and collectibles purchase, do not involve an attorney, the Better Business Bureau, or the media (especially social media) until you have approached the dealer or auctioneer who sold you the item and discussed the problem. This sounds so obvious, but many collectors and investors who feel that they have been cheated will either refuse to talk to someone they believe is dishonest, or will assume that the seller will not want to help them. But most art and collectibles dealers are ethical, and also want a continuing relationship with their customers. Even those whose practices are not consistently ethical want to avoid trouble, and will work with a customer who seems to know what his or her rights are. So the very first thing someone should ask when facing a problem purchase is whether he or she has discussed the problem with the person from whom they bought the item.

Start the process by assembling your evidence. If the problem relates to authenticity, be prepared to explain why you believe the item to be suspect. If you believe the item was overpriced, collect relevant price information, and so on. Do your research. Arrange to share this information with the dealer and ask the dealer to show you his or her backup for the representations made about the item. In appropriate cases, you may wish to retain an expert to review the evidence, either on your own or in conjunction with the dealer (see the following section on "Arbitration"). Just remember what was covered in chapters 2 and 3—the dealer owes you certain warranties, and for at least four years (the statute of limitations under the Uniform Commercial Code [UCC]), the dealer must be prepared to prove that the warranties were met.

The next thing to remember is not to expect a dealer to immediately rescind the purchase and refund your purchase price. Depending on the item, rescission can be extremely burdensome to a dealer. An art gallery that is no longer showing a particular artist does not want to buy back one of that artist's works. Even dealers in more liquid items such as rare coins do not want to lose the profit on the initial sale, and if the market value of the item has fallen since the original purchase, a buy-back can result in a substantial loss. Remember also that dealers and auctioneers may protect themselves through disclaimers of warranties in the purchase contracts or terms and conditions of sale. So full refunds are rarely encountered unless the amount is insubstantial, the dealer agrees that the item is fake or was misdescribed, or you make a particularly compelling case and the dealer does not want to fight with you about it. The dealer may, however, offer to buy the item back, but at the "wholesale" price the dealer would normally pay for the item. Or the dealer may agree to accept the item for consignment, to be sold to another customer on your behalf. Generally, should you choose to sell directly to the dealer, you may get slightly more than wholesale because the dealer wants you to be totally satisfied, and dealers and auction houses often waive commissions for consignment sales by unhappy customers.

After conferring with the dealer, you may decide that you are not entitled to a refund after all. Many investors complain when the market value of their purchase declines, but few are entitled to a refund solely because of that—you wouldn't share your profits with the dealer, so why would the dealer share your losses? Likewise, collectors who become disenchanted with a particular artist will demand their money back as though the dealer gave a lifetime buyback guarantee. Some do give such guarantees—most don't. Art and collectible items are rich with subjective descriptions, as well as associations that derive from the *buyer* and were not part of the *seller's* warranties. These are situations where dealers simply do not have legal (or moral) obligations to their customers. And a certain degree of personal responsibility attaches to major purchases, too. We have spent much of our careers representing both dealers and individual investors, and have found that where each approaches the other in good faith and with a desire to resolve a problem, most of the time there is no need for anyone else's intervention.

ARBITRATION

If the dealer will not recognize your problem, or you believe that the dealer's offer is unreasonably low, you should suggest that the dispute be arbitrated. Arbitration is a very effective remedy in art and collectibles cases for several reasons. First, it is fast, with most simple cases reaching an award (ready to be confirmed as a court judgment) in a matter of weeks or, at most, months. Litigation is far slower, and often you are hostage to court backlogs and attorney schedules. Second, arbitration panels can include experts in particular fields, so that disputed matters of authenticity and market value can be heard by knowledgeable persons rather than lay judges or jurors. Third, in practically every case arbitration is far less expensive than litigation. Fourth, it is final, with the loser having virtually no chance of successfully appealing an award (and thereby delaying its implementation).

The American Arbitration Association (AAA) handles arbitration cases through regional offices across the country, and among its list of available arbitrators are people from the art community. Another arbitration provider is Judicial Arbitration and Mediation Services (JAMS), which likewise serves claimants throughout the United States, and is known for the fact that most of its arbitrators previously served as judges. If you want to ensure in advance that disputes will be arbitrated you may place words such as the following in the contract:

> Any controversy or claim arising out of or relating to this transaction shall be settled by arbitration in accordance with the Commercial

> Arbitration Rules of the American Arbitration Association [AAA] conducted in [city, state]. Judgment upon the award rendered by the Arbitrator may be entered in any court having jurisdiction thereof.

If there is no written contract, or if the contract does not provide for arbitration, the parties can nevertheless agree to AAA arbitration once their dispute has arisen. The AAA has submission forms that both parties sign to accept arbitration of their dispute.

Recently, a specialized arbitration forum was created for disputes relating to art, namely the Court of Arbitration for Art (CAfA). This is based in The Netherlands, but conducts arbitration proceedings worldwide (Armen is on its list of US-based arbitrators). If rare coins are involved, check to see if the dealer belongs to the Professional Numismatists Guild (PNG). PNG is a well-established organization of major coin professionals worldwide, and its members must agree to arbitrate their disputes with customers through PNG. Other organizations in art and collectibles fields have similar requirements. When doing business with one of these dealers, you know that you have the option to arbitrate.

Arbitrations generally are before a sole arbitrator or panel of three arbitrators. In some cases, the parties can agree on a particular person to act as sole arbitrator, and will accept his or her determination as final. In other cases, the parties will each appoint an arbitrator and the two party-appointed arbitrators will appoint the third, or "umpire." AAA provides lists of available arbitrators in specialized fields, and in the case of PNG the arbitrators are appointed by PNG itself from among its membership. Arbitrations are informal, in the sense that they are conducted in offices rather than courtrooms and lack many of the rules and procedures that encumber litigation. For example, rules of evidence are somewhat relaxed, and arbitrators are more likely to accept hearsay or unauthenticated documentary evidence than would a court. With industry professionals as arbitrators, it is also unnecessary to educate the arbitrators about the type of item that is at issue. This means that the arbitrators can get to the point and not spend time getting up to speed.

In our experience, the results of arbitrations are at least as fair to both sides as those in litigations, and investors or collectors need not be concerned that dealer-arbitrators will be biased in favor of their fellow dealers. Dealers who serve as arbitrators generally have the highest ethical standards, and they also have a long-term view of their industries, which includes a desire that disputes be fairly handled. As PNG's Legal Counsel for nearly thirty years, Armen has observed many rare coin–related arbitrations and they are extremely fair.

LITIGATION

Arbitration is fine for most disputes. However, if a dispute involves a great deal of money, or if it is likely to involve investigation of facts or complex legal issues, it may be safer to go through the court process. Judges can order recalcitrant parties to produce documents and witnesses, and while the "relaxed" attitude of arbitration is sometimes just what the parties need, in some cases firm principles must be applied to one or both sides in order to achieve justice swiftly and fairly. Moreover, arbitration is not available if both parties don't agree to it. In cases where one or both dealer and customer refuse to arbitrate, litigation may be the only choice.

We always advise collectors or investors to move quickly once they determine that a negotiated or arbitrated settlement is impossible. Dealers who do not deliver goods that they sell, or who overprice investment items or falsely represent their authenticity, quality, or grade, usually do not stay in business very long. And such dealers generally attract many unhappy customers and creditors, and are faced with a number of lawsuits in different federal and state courts around the country. Some even end up in bankruptcy, or as a defendant in government enforcement proceedings. It is unfortunate, but in most cases the customers who strike first get the best treatment from the legal system.

As with the purchase of art and collectibles, litigation is a business transaction that should be carefully studied. Before filing suit, you and your attorney must be on the same page regarding fees and costs. You should demand an estimate, including how much will be due from you at various stages along the way. Retainers should be carefully explained, particularly as to whether any or all of them are nonrefundable in the event the case settles or you decide to switch attorneys. And any contingent fee agreement should be in writing and should provide for who pays out-of-pocket expenses such as expert and stenographer fees. There is simply no substitute for hiring an attorney with knowledge of art and collectibles. This is an area of expertise that takes years to develop, and by hiring such an attorney, you will have all the benefits of that expertise and experience. Competent attorneys from outside the field have to spend a great deal of time familiarizing themselves with its unique business practices and legal rules, and even if they learn everything they need to know for the case, this knowledge will come at a high price to you.

Do not expect quick results from litigation. Court congestion and attorney schedules often create frustrating delays. Moreover, defendants often find ways of slowing down even the most determined plaintiff's team. And the process of discovering information from one another, through document requests, interrogatories, and depositions, nearly always will take months, if not years. It helps greatly if a plaintiff is focused, does his or her homework, and interacts intelligently with the attorney about the material facts and his or her litigation objectives. That way, unnecessary attorney work and expense are limited, and the issues in the case are narrowed.

Finally, be prepared to discuss settlement throughout the litigation process. Don't fight lawsuits "on principle." These types of principles can be very expensive, and we all have better things to do with our time and energy (even we attorneys!). Litigation can provide the pressure needed to move parties to settle. And judges, looking to remove one case from their workload, will often add more pressure on the parties. Sometimes it is the defendant that moves, sometimes the plaintiff, usually both. By never losing sight of the "value" of your case, you can get what you want with the least possible pain and delay.

COPYRIGHT DISPUTES

Owners of registered copyrights can pursue their claims in federal courts or arbitration (pursuant to an agreement). A prevailing copyright owner often even receives their attorneys' fees. But despite the fact that a copyright owner may recover their attorneys' fees at the successful conclusion of litigation, the up-front cost and extensive timelines associated with litigation, or even arbitration, is commonly prohibitive to owners who want to protect their rights in works that may not generate much in terms of funds for the creator.

Therefore, the Copyright Alternative in Small-Claims Enforcement Act of 2019 (the CASE Act) was enacted by Congress. Intended, at the time of writing, to be in operation by December 27, 2021, the CASE Act requires the Copyright Office to provide an alternative to the federal courts wherein three Copyright Claims Officers will serve as judges to hear disputes under the Copyright Act and the Digital Millennium Copyright Act (DMCA). CASE offers limited statutory damages and attorneys' fees: $15,000 per timely registered work, damage awards capped at a total of $30,000, and attorneys' fees are only awarded in cases of bad faith conduct or a frivolous claim. Note that at $15,000 per work but a total cap of $30,000, a CASE panel is not only undesirable if you expect larger damages but also if you have a claim for infringement of more than two works.

The CASE panel is entirely voluntary, meaning that when a claimant initiates an action and serves it on a respondent, the respondent can choose not to participate. This is similar to arbitration, except that as of yet, no one is including provisions to submit any copyright disputes to a CASE panel. Unlike arbitration, because damages are so limited, it is unlikely CASE provisions will begin to appear in contracts; it would only benefit a copyright owner if they anticipate multiple people infringing their work but almost always under conditions where a court or jury would only award minimal statutory damages. For example, an artist creating a website that displays his or her artwork may have many copyright disputes with individuals copying the image from the website in a manner that technically infringes the artist's rights but would result in minimal damages. Such an artist may benefit by including in their terms and conditions a provision that all visitors consent to resolve copyright disputes through a CASE panel (provided their art is not selling at prices that could result in a damages award beyond $15,000 per work).

Absent an agreement, if a respondent chooses not to participate in a CASE proceeding, the claimant must then proceed in court if they wish to proceed at all. Because the CASE proceedings are expected to be more time and cost efficient than litigation, respondents that believe they have a valid fair use defense and wish to make those arguments rather than settle quickly will likely consent to a CASE proceeding. Unfortunately, we may see some respondents refusing to participate based on a strategy that the claimant does not have the financial resources to proceed in court and therefore a refusal at the CASE stage would end the dispute.

CASE panel decisions will be subject to the same grounds for judicial appeal as provided under the Federal Arbitration Act; the appellant may only challenge the decision on the basis of fraud, corruption, or other misconduct. However, the CASE Act also provides a losing party the ability to request first that the panel reconsider the case, and second that the Register of Copyrights review whether the panel abused its discretion if it refuses to reconsider.

REMEDIES

Whether negotiating, arbitrating, or litigating, it is important to know what remedies are available against dealers in art and collectibles cases. The available remedies depend, in large part, on the type of unlawful conduct the plaintiff is asserting and the statute or legal rule on which the claim is based.

Breach of Contract: Rescission

One category of claims is breach of contract, which includes breach of warranty. Contract remedies generally seek to place the aggrieved plaintiff where he or she would have been had there been no breach. For the types of breaches described in chapters 1 and 2—that is, sale of unauthentic or improperly described art or collectible items—the most common remedy is rescission. Rescission is reversal of the contract—return of the goods in exchange for refund of the purchase price. The dealer, having made the warranty, must suffer having the tainted item back.

Even where the market value of the item has fallen since the date of purchase, the courts have said that it is not unfair to require the dealer to return the full purchase price, the assumption being that there would never have been a sale in the first place if the buyer had known the truth about the item. On the other hand, it is quite unusual in a contract or warranty case for the plaintiff to recover *more* than the contract price, such as pre-judgment interest, attorneys' fees, or multiple damages. And consequential damages—that is, the lost profit that would have been made had the item been as described (or had the money been invested elsewhere)—are not awarded either.

Common Law Torts: Damages

In some cases, breach of warranty claims aren't made, either because the four-year statute of limitations has expired, or because the warranties were ambiguous or disclaimed. In such cases, and others where more serious wrongdoing took place, buyers claim under tort law. Torts include fraud, breach of fiduciary duty, negligence, and product liability. With art and collectibles, the most often seen tort claim is common law fraud. By asserting that the dealer knowingly deceived him or her regarding a material aspect of the purchase, the buyer makes available certain rights and remedies that do not exist in breach of warranty claims.

First, the claim can be brought more than four years after the purchase. The limits in UCC § 2-725 do not apply to fraud claims, and most state's laws incorporate a "discovery rule" into their statutes of limitations. Thus, the limitations period begins only when plaintiffs discover that they have been defrauded or in the exercise of reasonable diligence should have discovered it. The best practical example of this principle is *Rosen v. Spanierman,*[1] discussed in chapter 2. While the plaintiffs' breach of warranty claim relating to a fake painting was dismissed because the UCC's four-year statute of limitations had expired and the "future performance" exception did not apply, the plaintiffs' fraud claim was allowed to continue because under New York law (N.Y. C.P.L.R. § 213(8), 213(f)), fraud claims may be brought on the later of (1) six years from the date of the fraud, or (2) two years from the date the fraud was discovered or could have been discovered. In *Rosen,* the lawsuit was filed nineteen years after the fraud was committed, but less than two years from when it was discovered. Note that courts will not extend limitations periods indefinitely for plaintiffs who have not been diligent. A case in point is *Hope v. Klabal,*[2] where a buyer of more than ten million dollars in artworks was found to be less than diligent in learning that the art was overpriced—the court emphasizing her sophistication as a businessperson, and the ready availability of independent experts to appraise the works she was buying.

Second, a fraud claim can be asserted by someone other than the original purchaser, provided that the dealer could reasonably have foreseen that this type of person would obtain the product. For example, the wholesale distributor of a print might prepare brochures containing representations, and then sell the prints and brochures to retail galleries. If a retail buyer learns that some of the representations were false, he or she can sue the gallery for breach of warranty. But what if the gallery is out of business? While breach of warranty is only available

[1] Rosen v. Spanierman, 894 F.2d 28 (2d Cir. 1990).

[2] Hope v. Klabal, 457 F.3d 784 (8th Cir. 2006).

against the gallery, a fraud claim might be made against the distributor who knowingly prepared and disseminated the false brochures.

Third, proving fraud will entitle the buyer to a wider scope of damages. It is not uncommon for courts to award buyers *the greater of* rescission plus interest or the value of the item had it been described correctly. In the case of an investor in art who was fraudulently sold a fake, the court stated that rescission was not good enough because the market value of that artist's genuine works had increased dramatically since the date of purchase. The damages would be the difference in present value between the fake and the original. In addition, in the fraud cases the chances of recovering consequential damages and attorneys' fees are greater.

STATUTORY VIOLATIONS: DIFFERING REMEDIES

A number of different federal and state statutes provide rights of action for buyers of art and collectibles, and there are some definite benefits to asserting claims under these statutes. The three relevant federal statutes are the Telemarketing Act, the Lanham Act, and the Hobby Protection Act, all of which were discussed in earlier chapters.

The Telemarketing Act allows individuals to bring lawsuits for unfair or deceptive practices that previously only the Federal Trade Commission (FTC) or state attorney general could bring. Provided that the plaintiff meets the Telemarketing Rule's threshold of fifty thousand dollars in damages, and the transaction involves interstate activity (i.e., an out-of-state dealer or supplier), suit can be brought in federal court for damages, including attorneys' fees. The plaintiff must notify the FTC in writing before filing suit, and the FTC has the right to intervene and take over the case, presumably if it determines that the public interest is at stake.

The Lanham Act is the federal unfair trade practices statute, authorizing suits in federal court where the origin, quality/grade, or provenance of goods is misrepresented to consumers. While the Lanham Act is often used to combat "knock-offs" of trademarked items such as Rolex watches, it is equally applicable to art or collectible items whose value depends so much on the correctness of such representations. The Lanham Act allows consumers to recover double or triple damages in cases of knowing and willful conduct by the dealer, and also allows recovery of attorneys' fees. It is a powerful tool for consumer protection.

Finally, the Hobby Protection Act, discussed in chapter 16, allows purchasers of replica coins or political memorabilia not clearly marked as such to sue for damages and recover their attorneys' fees as well.

State statutes also add to the remedies available to buyers of art and collectibles. In addition to the rights of the states themselves to bring suit (see chapter 17), private rights of action are created in most state's consumer protection laws. The New York and California laws described in chapters 1 and 2 provide some rights specifically in the areas of fine art prints and autographed sports memorabilia, but in other collecting areas the general consumer protection laws will also support claims. The only prerequisites for a right of action under state consumer laws are that some part of the transaction has taken place in the state, and that the consumer attempted to resolve the dispute with the dealer by sending a written claim more than thirty days before filing suit.

One benefit of asserting private rights under federal or state statutes is that these rights cannot be disclaimed or waived, unlike the right to bring breach of warranty actions. For example, Texas Deceptive Trade Practices-Consumer Protection Act § 17.42 essentially eliminates any waiver by consumers, by requiring that waivers (1) be in writing and signed by the consumer, (2) that the consumer not be in a disparate bargaining position with the dealer and be represented by an attorney of his or her own choosing, (3) that the waiver be conspicuous and have a heading "waiver of Consumer Rights," and (4) that the waiver read essentially as follows:

> I waive my rights under the Deceptive Trade Practices-Consumer Protection Act, Section 17.41 et seq., Business & Commerce Code, a law that gives consumers special rights and protections. After consultation with an attorney of my own selection, I voluntarily consent to this waiver.

So even after agreeing to a disclaimer of express and implied warranties, a buyer of art and collectibles retains his or her rights under consumer protection statutes. Another benefit is a generally longer statute of limitations, because of the "discovery rules." And perhaps most important is the ability to recover multiple damages and attorneys' fees, which gives consumers greater leverage in negotiating a settlement.

SUMMARY

If you do find yourself in a dispute concerning a purchase or sale of art or collectibles, consider the following:

- First, assemble your evidence and know what remedies are available (and what you want), which may include:
  - Rescission of the contract (the seller takes the item back and refunds the money);
  - Payment of the difference between the amount paid and the reduced value of the item;
  - Statutory damages, either in cases of consumer fraud or a flat rate award for each instance of copyright infringement.
- First try to approach the buyer/seller to negotiate directly. Most dealers want to find an ethical solution but they may too have been damaged and want to mitigate their loss.
- If the parties cannot resolve the dispute themselves, arbitration may be an effective solution, allowing a panel of persons (experienced in both law and sometimes even the particular art and collectibles industry) to issue an award much faster than a court case. Many sale and consignment agreements include an arbitration provision.
- While the court system moves slower, it can be more effective in issuing preliminary relief (such as preventing a party from moving, selling, or destroying an item before the case is resolved).
- Legal action carries financial burdens (as well as costing time, energy, and stress) and winning a financial judgment does not ensure the opposing party will have the money to pay it (even if the prevailing party is entitled to their attorney's fees, those are usually paid to attorneys throughout the dispute and added to the judgment). Therefore, legal action should be pursued as a business decision, not on principle.

17

The Federal Trade Commission and Other Government Agencies

Collectors and investors who believe that they have been cheated often seek the government's assistance in recovering their money and putting the bad guys out of business. In the art and collectibles world, the leading federal regulatory agency is the Federal Trade Commission (FTC). On the state level, the various attorney general's offices handle hundreds, if not thousands, of complaints relating to art and collectibles each year.

THE FEDERAL TRADE COMMISSION

The FTC is empowered, among other things, to enforce the FTC Act § 5, which prohibits "unfair or deceptive acts or practices in commerce." Misrepresentations of material facts made to induce the purchase of goods or services violate § 5. In the 1980s, the FTC began to be interested in practices in the art and collectibles fields, particularly the sale of fine art prints and rare coins as investments. Through its Bureau of Consumer Protection in Washington, DC, the FTC continues to investigate and prosecute dealers and others in these and other fields.

The FTC invites consumer complaints against retailers. However, the FTC does not resolve individual complaints. Rather, it looks for patterns of conduct that threaten *the public as a whole.* Therefore, the FTC typically will not commence an investigation on the basis of only one or two complaints. Those consumers will be referred to other dispute resolution mechanisms or advised to seek private remedies in court. In truly exceptional cases the FTC will, on its own initiative, investigate a company whose advertising and other practices may violate the FTC Act.

The standard the FTC applies under § 5 is one of deception: would a reasonable person of average intelligence have relied upon, and been misled by, the representations or omissions made by the dealer? As with fraud claims generally, the misrepresentations must be material, and must cause consumer harm in the absence of market declines or other factors. The FTC's specific focus over the years has been improper marketing of speculative, high-markup items as safe, low-risk investments. An extended quotation from an opinion of the Eighth Circuit Court of Appeals in *FTC v. Security Rare Coin & Bullion Corp.*[1] shows the reasoning behind FTC prosecution of one collectibles dealer:

> Security Coin was in the business of selling rare coins, a highly technical and specialized commodity unfamiliar to most consumers. Security Coin marketed foreign and domestic coins through telephone solicitation, direct mail, and advertisements in its own financial publications and in national newspapers. Security Coin represented its coins as excellent low-risk investments sold at or near market value with superior liquidity and profit potential. Security Coin sought to overcome consumer resistance and concern about risk by heavily promoting the existence of a "buy-back" policy, under which it would repurchase coins at a discount from its current sales prices. These promotions resulted in substantial sales of coins.
>
> Security Coin graded the value of its own coins and arbitrarily marked up the price of the coins sold to consumers two or three times the wholesale price. Because the coins would have to double or triple in value before any gain could be realized, Security Coin's representations as to their investment value were fraudulent.
>
> . . .
>
> To satisfy the reliance requirement in actions brought under . . . the Act, the FTC need merely show that the misrepresentations or

[1] FTC v. Security Rare Coin & Bullion Corp., 931 F.2d 1312 (8th Cir. 1991).

> omissions were of the kind usually relied upon by reasonable and prudent persons, that they were widely disseminated, and that the injured consumers actually purchased the defendants' products. Security made credible and persuasive misrepresentations concerning the coins' allegedly low prices, high profit potential, and low risk. These are key factors in a consumer's decision to purchase coins for investment purposes. We agree with the district court and the FTC that it was reasonable for consumers entering this specialized and technical market to rely on the representations of an apparently reputable firm staffed by experts and specializing in such investments.

When debating implementation of the Telemarketing Act in 1995, FTC representatives sought to require that dealers in "tangible assets" (which includes art and collectible items) disclose to customers the amount they actually paid for the items they sell, and also disclose "all material facts" before accepting any money from the customer. Although the final version of the Telemarketing Rule did not contain specific regulations aimed at tangible assets dealers, the FTC showed its particular concern for this area of the investment marketplace.

The FTC has no criminal jurisdiction, but instead proceeds through civil enforcement actions in federal district court. Quite frequently, where the FTC fears dissipation of assets and wants to prevent additional consumer fraud, it will ask the court for an immediate injunction against misrepresentations, a freeze of the dealer's assets, and the appointment of a receiver to manage the dealer's business. Armen has served as a receiver in an FTC action, and also has been appointed special counsel at the request of the FTC in another case.

Ultimately, FTC complaints seek permanent injunctions against unlawful behavior as well as monetary redress to consumers who have been harmed by that behavior. As a result of FTC action, many unscrupulous art and collectibles investment firms have been shut down, and their principals punished. Unfortunately, the FTC has not been particularly successful at providing monetary redress in art and collectibles cases, primarily because the principals are bankrupt and "judgment-proof" by the time the FTC gets to them. And a 2021 US Supreme Court decision reinterpreted § 5 of the FTC Act as not authorizing monetary redress in consumer cases, a decision that sent shockwaves through the

FTC and may result in congressional action to expressly authorize monetary relief in FTC § 5 cases. While we have advised many consumer clients to notify the FTC about their unsatisfactory experiences with art and collectibles dealers, we don't recommend starting with the FTC to resolve a specific dispute or get a refund.

STATE ATTORNEYS GENERAL

At the state level, attorneys general enforce state consumer protection laws, such as Massachusetts Chapter 93A and Texas Deceptive Trade Practice-Consumer Protection Act, Tex. Business & Commerce Law § 17.41 *et seq.* These laws are sometimes referred to as "baby FTC Acts" because they usually overlap with the protections provided by § 5 of the FTC Act. In addition, in states such as New York and California that have specific statutes relating to the protection of art and collectibles buyers, the attorneys general of those states are charged with protecting the public interest. Unfair or deceptive practices such as would violate the FTC Act also probably would be actionable under the state equivalents.

The trick is to get a state agency interested in your problem. If the dealer is located out of state, as is frequently the case in investment fraud cases, an attorney general's office might not want to prosecute, although this is changing with the Telemarketing Act, which authorizes state attorneys general to sue in federal court on behalf of its residents even where the defendant is elsewhere. State agencies are closer and more accessible than the FTC and are far more likely to intervene in particular cases involving their residents. An attorney general's consumer protection division will forward consumer complaints to the dealer involved and request a response from the dealer. Dealers that refuse to cooperate, or whose responses are unsatisfactory, may be investigated further. States have powers similar to the FTC with respect to freezing assets, enjoining unlawful conduct, and providing consumer redress.

In art market states such as New York and California, as was discussed in earlier chapters, additional legislation exists specifically addressing problems in the art and collectibles businesses, and generally those laws are enforced by the state attorney general. For example, the New York attorney general can sue to get an injunction against a dealer's violation of the disclosure laws for autographed sports collectibles, fine prints and sculptures, as well as for restitution payments to injured customers, and civil penalties of one thousand dollars per violation (five hundred dollars in the case of fine prints or sculptures).

Finally, local agencies such as the New York Department of Consumer Affairs regulate practices in the art and collectibles fields. New York's Auction Regulations, which were mentioned briefly in chapter 9, are issued and enforced by that organization.

SUMMARY

Should you report a dealer to a government agency?

- The Federal Trade Commission (FTC) investigates and prosecutes dealers who make misrepresentations of material facts to induce the purchase of goods and services.
- The FTC focuses on dealers who sell art and collectibles using misrepresentations as to the riskiness or investment potential of the items.
- The FTC will not resolve your individual complaints, but alerting the FTC to a dealer you believe fraudulently induced you to buy goods may assist them in pursuing a dealer who has a pattern of defrauding the general public.
- State attorneys general also enforce consumer protection laws at the state level. These attorneys general don't usually require the dealer's fraudulent activity to be as extensive before they get involved, as long as the dealer is also located in their state.

PART 6

Taxation of Art and Collectibles

Chapter 13 discussed how the burgeoning online market has affected sales and use taxes; chapter 18 provides a more comprehensive discussion of sales, use, and income taxes as concerning art and collectibles. This part of the book also discusses the issue of art and collectibles placed in individual retirement accounts and the subsequent recordkeeping required.

18

Sales, Use, and Income Taxes

There is very little we do in the United States today that is not somehow affected by the tax laws. Buying and selling art and collectibles is no exception. An understanding of basic principles of state and local sales and use tax, income tax, and estate tax will not only assure compliance with the law but may save you money as well. Of course, be warned that tax laws change quite often and that differences in geography, income, and overall portfolio may change the effect of taxes considerably. You should always consult a competent attorney or tax advisor to update yourself and to tailor any tax strategies to your particular situation.

SALES TAX

Most US state and local governments impose a sales tax on retailers for the privilege of retailing tangible personal property. The tax is usually a percentage of the gross sale price of the goods, and is remitted by the dealer along with a sales tax return. While the dealer is actually liable for the sales tax, a nearly universal practice is to pass the cost of sales taxes on to the retail customer. In a typical over-the-counter sale of art and collectibles, the dealer will add the appropriate sales tax to the invoice price of the coins.

The taxable event for a sales tax is an in-state retail sale. This leads to two common exemptions to sales taxes. First, a sales tax is not due on wholesale (dealer-to-dealer) sales, but only where the buyer holds a valid resale permit or certificate from that state or another state. Second, sales by out-of-state retailers are traditionally exempt from a sales tax if (1) the customer orders goods directly from the retailer and (2) the goods are shipped from outside the state and no in-state branch, office, outlet, or other place of business of the seller participates in the sale. However, as discussed more fully in chapter 13 and later in this chapter, since the Supreme Court's *Wayfair* opinion in 2018, approximately thirty states have followed South Dakota's example and taken steps to undermine the out-of-state exemption by requiring such sellers to collect use taxes.

In certain states, some sales of rare coins are specifically exempted from a sales tax for various reasons. States that do not apply a sales tax to the sale of money exempt sales of "coins of the realm," defined as coins that remain legal tender of the United States or a foreign government. Others do not tax investment purchases, and assume that "bulk" purchases of more than $1,500 are for investment. However, in most states, unless the sale falls into one of the common exemptions, a sales tax will apply.

Dealers occasionally ask buyers of expensive items whether they wish goods to be shipped to a friend or relative in a neighboring state, thereby relieving the dealer of the responsibility to charge the sales tax. If the item is actually shipped, a sales tax exemption may apply. *Never* take the item with you and allow an empty package to be shipped out of state. If a dealer wishes to cheat the state, you shouldn't voluntarily participate in the scheme. And with recent legal developments relating to use taxes, it has become much more difficult for either the seller or the buyer to avoid state tax obligations.

USE TAX

States have become much more aggressive in enforcing their right to collect a use tax on certain sales, including in the art and collectibles marketplace. While a sales tax is triggered by a dealer's exercise of the privilege of doing retail business in a state, a use tax is based entirely on the purchase of property for use in the taxing state. The taxable event is the purchase and use, not the sale, and the tax is due from the buyer, not the seller. A use tax is far more difficult to predict than a sales tax. For one thing, the sale need not take place in the taxing state, provided that the buyer resides there. This means that mail order purchases that are exempt from a sales tax nevertheless are subject to a use tax. States are quite candid in saying that a use tax levels the playing field between local, in-state, dealers who have to pay a sales tax and their out-of-state competitors who don't. Generally, states hold dealers responsible for collecting and remitting a use tax on behalf of their customers, and for all practical purposes states will not attempt to collect back taxes from individual customers if the dealer itself is solvent. However, the liability is there, and it can continue indefinitely if the unwary buyer does not file a use tax return.

The states with the largest collectibles markets, such as New York and California, historically have led the way on use taxes. They stipulated that dealers with an in-state office, agent, warehouse, or other permanent physical presence have a close enough "nexus" with their states to require collecting use taxes on all sales to their residents. But these states have also aggressively audited dealers with no permanent physical presence there, even dealers who just attend local art fairs or coin shows. For example, in July 1995, California's Board of Equalization announced that attending a single retail coin show in California might create nexus, causing the American Numismatic Association to move its 1996 early spring fair from Santa Clara to Tucson, Arizona. In *Orvis Co. v. Tax Tribunal*,[1] New York's highest court ruled that Orvis, a Vermont mail order seller of outdoor equipment, acquired nexus with New York after Orvis personnel made twelve trips to New York City over a three-year period to monitor product displays at independent stores that carry Orvis products. Orvis's personnel did not attend shows or even make a single sale in New York.

While states realize the dangers of discouraging out-of-state dealers from doing business there, the difficulties that the states face in collecting use taxes from buyers who fail to report purchases makes the potential for additional revenue through the sellers irresistible. And the US Supreme Court opened the door to use tax collection quite widely in its June 2018 decision in *South Dakota v. Wayfair, Inc.*,[2] which eliminated any "physical presence" requirement for application of a state's use tax and permitted states to tax purchases where the seller's only connection to

---

1 Orvis Co. v. Tax Tribunal, 86 N.Y.2d 165 (1995).

2 South Dakota v. Wayfair, Inc., 585 U.S. ___, 138 S.Ct. 2080 (2018).

the state was a threshold amount of mail order or Internet sales there. Within the first two years after the *Wayfair* decision, more than thirty states amended their laws accordingly. It is difficult, if not impossible, to avoid use taxes for sales of art and collectible items, except in unusual circumstances that are beyond the scope of this book.

INCOME TAX

Net income from the sale of art and collectibles is taxable, but not until the item is sold or otherwise disposed of for value. For some people, this makes art and collectibles a preferred investment vehicle over stocks, whose dividends are taxed annually even if they are in the form of new stock and not cash. An investor can defer taxable gains until a time of his or her own choosing. However, there's a considerable difference between the 28 percent long-term capital gains rate for art or collectible items (the Internal Revenue Service [IRS] lumps them together as "collectibles") and the 15 percent to 20 percent rate for other capital assets. The relative tax advantages of art and collectibles vis-à-vis other forms of investment are beyond the scope of this book, and you should seek advice specially tailored to your financial portfolio from financial professionals to make such decisions.

For purposes of this book, the key income tax aspects of purchases and sales of art and collectibles relate to the treatment of expenses and losses, and depend largely on whether, for tax purposes, you are a collector, an investor, or a dealer. Sounds simple enough, but many people spend a lot of time and effort arguing with the IRS and state taxing authorities over this characterization, because the tax consequences of each can be quite different.

Collectors, who buy and sell coins primarily for personal pleasure, are the most tax-*disadvantaged* class. They must pay tax on income they earn from their coins but cannot deduct net losses they might have from coin sales. They cannot deduct any expenses relating to their collection, such as insurance, security, membership dues for coin clubs, and subscriptions to numismatic periodicals, but can offset these expenses against any net income they declare from the sale of coins. Unfortunately, even this benefit is substantially limited because it comprises a "miscellaneous" itemized deduction on Schedule A subject to the 2 percent adjusted gross income floor. In other words, unless the collector itemizes deductions, and the collector's total miscellaneous expenses exceed 2 percent of adjusted gross income, there is no benefit. Collectors are entitled to treat their coins as capital assets after a one-year holding period, but the difference between tax rates for capital gains and ordinary income is not as great today as it has been in the past.

Investors fare slightly better. They can deduct expenses relating to their art and collectibles portfolios, but not net losses from sales. However, the IRS makes it more and more difficult to qualify as an investor, clearly preferring to characterize everyone interested in art and collectibles as a collector. The key is whether the taxpayer is engaged in the activity for profit or for enjoyment. Taxpayers who show a profit from their activities for three of the past five years are presumed to be engaged in those activities for profit, although the IRS has the right to rebut that presumption. The IRS has published nine relevant factors in determining whether a taxpayer is a collector or an investor:

- Does the time and effort put into the activity indicate an intention to make a profit?
- Do you depend on income from the activity?
- If there are losses, are they due to circumstances beyond your control or did they occur in the start-up phase of the business?
- Have you changed methods of operation to improve profitability?
- Do you have the knowledge needed to carry on the activity as a successful business?
- Have you made a profit in similar activities in the past?
- Does the activity make a profit in some years?
- Do you expect to make a profit in the future from the appreciation of assets used in the activity?
- Does the activity provide non-financial benefits, such as recreation?[3]

Taking these one at a time, here's what taxpayers need to consider when applying for investor status:

1. The taxpayer's time and effort in carrying out the activity. Does the amount of time the taxpayer spends on his or her collection indicate a desire to earn a profit from the activity, rather than simply passively holding the items and enjoying profits if they come?

---

[3] 26 C.F.R. § 1.183-2(b).

2. The taxpayer's financial status. Although other substantial sources of income to the taxpayer do not preclude an activity from being considered for-profit, they may indicate the activity is a hobby, and that the existence or nonexistence of profits is of little significance to the taxpayer.

3. The relative amounts of the profits and losses. IRS Regs. Sec. 1.183-2(b)(7) states, "The amount of profits in relation to the amount of losses incurred, and in relation to the amount of the taxpayer's investment and the value of the assets used in the activity, may provide useful criteria in determining the taxpayer's intent." When taxpayers seek to deduct losses from their art and collectibles investment activities against non-collection-related income, the IRS scrutinizes those very carefully to see if they are consistent with a profit motive.

4. How the taxpayer carries on the activity. The IRS wants to see that the taxpayer is behaving in a businesslike manner. In the case of art and collectibles investors, does the taxpayer maintain books and records showing profits and losses on particular items, and does the investor change his or her strategies and behaviors in response to such profits and losses? Or does the taxpayer merely collect what he or she finds interesting, and not what might prove to be profitable in the future? A comprehensive study of dozens of Tax Court cases on the hobby loss deduction has shown that only once has a taxpayer succeeded when "failing" this particular factor.

5. The taxpayer's expertise. Someone seeking a profit as an art or collectibles investor would be expected to have extensive knowledge of the relevant marketplace, having studied the price trends and sought advice from experts in the field. Subscriptions to market publications and relationships with acknowledged experts is a plus. This has been a pivotal factor, almost always existing in cases won by the taxpayer, and almost never existing in losing cases.

6. The taxpayer's success in other investment activities. The IRS recognizes that some taxpayers are adept at turning loss-making operations into profitable ones, and losses on some artworks or collectibles may not indicate the lack of a profit motive if the taxpayer can show that previous investments have turned profitable after a period of time. We'd expect the IRS would look for the taxpayer's investments in other collectibles—not securities or real estate—as the best evidence of this.

7. The taxpayer's history of income or losses from collectibles investing. As indicated above, IRC Sec. 183(d) says that if an activity has gross income for three or more of the past five years that exceeds the deductions attributable to the activity, the activity generally is *presumed* to be for-profit. The IRS has the right to try and rebut that presumption, but this is a crucial factor. Taxpayers who show a series of loss-making years are less favored.

8. An expectation that assets used in an activity may appreciate in value. Art and collectibles are a great example of assets that may be held for long-term appreciation, generating current expenses without current income. IRS Regs. Sec. 1.183-2(b)(4) says such appreciation may be considered in lieu of current profits.

9. Whether the activity provides recreation or involves "personal motives." This is a difficult one, because art or collectibles can be held for enjoyment, and the IRS will look to the above factors, as well as the types of items the investor purchases, and how the items are kept. For example, whether the investor displays the artwork at home or in the office, or keeps the rare coins in a safe deposit box, to see whether the collection is primarily for personal enjoyment, with profit motive being secondary. This factor has been significant in the reported cases, with only one taxpayer succeeding despite "failing" it. While owning art or collectibles brings a certain degree of pleasure, the cases won by the IRS often involve horse-breeding operations where the taxpayers also ride and care for the horses (enjoyable), and photography businesses where the taxpayers display their photographs, and other "businesses" where a family member is the only client, indicating more of a desire to support the family member than to operate a business.

Beyond collectors or investors, taxpayers who can establish that they buy and sell art or collectibles as part of a trade or business may acquire "dealer" status, enabling them to deduct expenses as well as net losses against their other income. As one might expect, the IRS is loath to treat a collector with other sources of income as a dealer. However, over the years the regulations in this area have been expanded so that it is not impossible for a serious enthusiast to qualify. The "for-profit" determination is similar to that described above for investors. Dealers pay tax at ordinary income rates, which again might be higher or lower than the

28 percent collectibles rate. Crucially, however, as a dealer the taxpayer may use losses to offset ordinary income from other sources.

One word about "wash sales." Many retailers offer tax breaks to collectors and investors whose tax basis in their portfolios is higher than their current value. The pitch is for the taxpayer to sell their portfolios to the dealer for a loss, take off the loss against capital gain income in that tax year, and then plow the proceeds of the sale back into more art or collectibles. The sale and tax loss part of the deal is fine. If the assets meet the holding period requirements, the losses can offset income. However, even by taking a small commission on the purchase, most retailers cannot acquire large portfolios without a ready customer. Consequently, we regularly see dealers offering to buy rare coin, stamp, or sports card portfolios that have declined in value, and then sell them back to the same customer thirty days later at their current market price, a transaction the IRS calls a "wash sale." Where the intent of the transaction is simply to generate a loss, the IRS will disallow that loss. Moreover, dealers who offer these deals generally take commissions on both ends, which would not be necessary were the prices fair to begin with.

LIKE-KIND EXCHANGES AND BARTER TRANSACTIONS

For many years, a popular marketing tool for retailers of art and collectibles was the "like-kind" exchange under Section 1031 of the Internal Revenue Code. That Code provision allowed investors in art and collectibles to trade items that had appreciated in value for items of the same "nature or character" without recognizing income or capital gains on the transaction. For investors interested in shifting from one area to another, this was a good tax-avoidance technique. However, for all intents and purposes the like-kind exchange was abolished for items of personal property by the 2017 Tax Cut and Jobs Act, although it remains available with respect to real property exchanges.

Unlike like-kind exchanges, barters are not a creation of the Internal Revenue Code, but rather comprise the age-old practice of people trading property based on each person's perception of market value, without cash changing hands. We discuss barter here because collectors and investors sometimes seek to avoid income tax on items that have appreciated in value by bartering with one another. While taxable gain on art and collectible items is not recognized until the items are sold, a barter is treated by the IRS as a "sale" because the taxpayer is disposing of the item in exchange for value. The celebrated artist Peter Max was indicted in 1996 for failing to report income from the barter of nearly one million dollars of artworks for the purchase of two residences.

One last point is that like-kind exchanges and barters are not necessarily exempt from sales or use taxes, and if a dealer is involved it is best to check on this before completing the deal.

ART AND COLLECTIBLES IN INDIVIDUAL RETIREMENT ACCOUNTS

Until the Reagan 1981 tax law took effect on January 1, 1982, art and collectibles (just "collectibles," in IRS parlance) could be purchased for placement in an individual retirement account (IRA) or other retirement plan, with all the tax benefits deriving from IRA eligibility. Since that date, purchase of art or collectibles by a retirement plan was deemed a distribution for tax purposes, effectively ending rollover of IRA account funds into art or collectibles. This change had a profound effect on the market in precious metal coins and other investment collectibles, as one of the primary motivations for purchase vanished, literally overnight. The IRS made clear that if such assets were already contained in retirement accounts, they could stay there with the same tax-deferred status they had previously. The question remains, however, can taxpayers roll over previously purchased art and collectibles without causing an involuntary distribution? The IRS has not given any clear answer to this question.

In any event, in 1986 Congress carved out a huge exception to the IRA ban with the introduction of the US Mint American Eagle program. US gold and silver coins dated 1986 and later may be purchased for retirement accounts, and Americans have purchased them in great numbers ever since. The exception even applies to US precious metal coins with substantial premiums, such as proof coins, somewhat inconsistent with Congress's otherwise strict prohibition of other "numismatic" coins in IRAs. And every year, bills are introduced to expand this exception to include all US legal tender coins, which would restore pre-1964 silver coins and pre-1933 gold coins to IRA eligibility.

While American Eagles are a good way of investing IRA funds in precious metals, they present special issues given the requirement that IRA assets must be held by a qualified trustee and not by the taxpayer directly. For securities this is simple, and even discount brokers offer IRA-custodian services for little or no charge. For a taxpayer wishing to buy gold or silver coins, however, the number of qualified custodians is small because of the security, insurance, and handling requirements of keeping thousands and thousands of precious metal items for individual investors. We've found that some precious metal dealers are not aware of these requirements, and it is also sometimes the case that investors simply pay for their metal purchases from an IRA account without telling the dealers. We've also seen art and collectibles dealers offering an end-around of the custodian requirement, having limited liability companies (LLCs) buy artworks or other collectibles, and then have the taxpayer's IRA purchase the LLCs. We're not sure about this latter strategy; the IRS doesn't like it and has challenged it, with some success. In a case where the taxpayer was the sole member of the LLC purchasing coins, the US Tax Court ruled that "Personal control over the IRA assets by the IRA owner is against the very nature of an IRA." The taxpayer was found to have taken a taxable distribution the moment she took physical possession of the coins purchased by the IRA-owned LLC.[4] Either way, to avoid an involuntary distribution, and the taxes and penalties flowing from it, do business only with experienced dealers and with the advice of a tax or legal professional.

RECORDKEEPING REQUIREMENTS IMPOSED BY THE UNITED STATES GOVERNMENT

For various reasons, anyone purchasing a sizable number of collectibles should keep detailed records regarding such purchases. The prices paid for each item should be detailed as well as the date of purchase, so that if the items are sold the gain (or loss) can be calculated and characterized—that is, as capital gain or ordinary income. In addition, if the taxpayer intends to deduct any expenses relating to collectibles,

---

4 Andrew McNulty and Donna McNulty v. Commissioner of Internal Revenue, 157 T.C. No. 10 (Nov. 18, 2021).

those expenses should be paid by check and an invoice or receipt obtained. If necessary, a note should state the purpose of the expense so that it can be proven to be within the expenses allowable by law.

Buyers of collectibles should realize that dealers also have documentation requirements imposed by the US government. Most dealers record every sale, no matter how small, and issue an invoice to the buyer. For cash purchases of art or collectibles for more than ten thousand dollars, or series of related cash purchases totaling more than that amount, dealers must file a report to the IRS on Form 8300 and send a copy to the buyer. This is part of the government's attempts to control tax evasion and money laundering. Reporting requirements also attach to sales of certain precious metals in large amounts. For example, sales of more than twenty-five South African Krugerrands or Canadian Maple Leaf coins, or one thousand dollars in face value of pre-1964 US silver coins, require the dealer purchasing these coins to file a Form 1099-B with the IRS, thereby informing the IRS of the gross sales proceeds paid to the customer. The list of coins requiring 1099-B reporting is small and somewhat arbitrary, and US gold and silver eagles are not on the list—sales of those coins in any amount do not require a report to the IRS. Reporting is not a bad thing, of course—income tax is due only on profits, and all law-abiding taxpayers should be paying their taxes regardless of whether someone reports their sales to the IRS. Nevertheless, many collectors and investors do not want to share their home addresses and Social Security numbers with precious metals dealers, which is necessary when selling reportable coins and bars.

Privacy concerns steer some buyers to nonreportable precious metals, and most precious metals dealers are well informed in these matters and can offer such items. This works for 1099-B—income tax—purposes, but buyers of art and collectibles should understand that governments all around the world, including the US government, are increasingly suspicious of the lack of transparency in art and collectibles markets, and how this is perceived to assist criminals involved in money laundering and terrorist financing. Some years ago, Congress, in the USA Patriot Act enacted after the 9/11 attacks, extended the reach of the Bank Secrecy Act to include dealers in precious metals and gemstones, thereby requiring those dealers to obtain more identifying information about their customers than previously had been required, and to file Suspicious Activity Reports (SARs) where transactions showed indicia of unlawful activities. For example, a SAR probably would have to be filed were a purchaser of precious metals to make payment from an account in Syria or Cuba, or from multiple accounts in countries other than the purchaser's country of residence. In the Anti-Money Laundering Act of 2020, similar requirements were extended to dealers in antiquities commencing January 1, 2021, although the relevant federal agencies have yet to finalize implementing regulations. Among the matters still unresolved by this legislation is the meaning of "antiquities," but it seems clear that the US government includes art in that definition. Here is part of a March 2021 release from the Financial Crimes Enforcement Network (FinCEN) concerning what FinCEN wants to see in SARs filed by antiquities dealers:

> Filers should provide any available details that may assist in the identification of (1) the objects connected to the financial transactions, (2) other transactions or proposed transactions that may involve antiquities or art, and (3) any other relevant information. Filers should provide all available details (such as names, identifiers, and contact information—including Internet Protocol (IP) and email addresses and phone numbers) regarding (1) the actual purchasers or sellers of the property, and their intermediaries or agents, (2) the volume and dollar amount of the transactions involving an entity that is—or may be functioning as—a dealer in antiquities or art, and (3) any beneficial owner(s) of entities (such as shell companies). In the case of stolen art or antiquities, filers should provide a detailed and specific description of the stolen item(s) and indicate whether photographs of the items are available. Filers should also provide information about the place(s) where the reported individuals or entities are operating.

As with the 1099-B requirements, such laws impose upon the privacy rights of all art and collectibles purchasers and sellers because of the unlawful actions of a few. This is difficult not only for collectors and investors who have to provide information, but also for dealers who must decide under what circumstances they must file SARs. For example, if a buyer asks to pay for a sizable art purchase with cryptocurrency, does the dealer file a SAR? Again, the law serves a worthy purpose, but at a very significant cost to privacy rights.

When buying or selling art or collectibles, all relevant records should be kept for at least ten years after the sale. This enables the collector/investor to fulfill all tax-related record-keeping requirements, and to comply with any government investigation of potential money laundering or other unlawful conduct. The more contemporaneous documentation of such things as state and local sales tax, commissions paid to an agent in connection with a purchase or sale, what items were being purchased or sold, and any other pertinent information should be itemized and in writing.

SUMMARY

Potential tax considerations to keep in mind when buying and selling art and collectibles include the following:

- A seller is now required to collect sales and use tax by most states, even when selling remotely.
- Income tax on art and collectibles is not due until the item is sold or disposed of, but is currently taxed at a higher rate than other capital assets.
- Like-kind exchanges are not currently recognized by the IRS, and a barter is considered a taxable "sale."
- The tax implications of buying and selling art and collectibles can vary based on whether you are doing so as a hobby or as an investment.
- With the exception of US gold and silver American Eagle coins dated 1986 and later, the circumstances under which art and collectibles may be held in an IRA varies by the item and when and for what purpose it was originally purchased.
- Detailed records of the purchase or sale of art and collectibles should be maintained for tax purposes.

Index

A

Abbott Laboratories v. Feinberg, 74–75
absentee bidding, 103
ACA Galleries v. Kinney, 16–17
advances, 90–91
American Arbitration Association (AAA), 169–170
American Numismatic Association (ANA), 87, 117, 189
Americans with Disabilities Act (ADA), 147–149
Anti-Money Laundering Act, 198
appreciation statistics, past, 58–60
arbitration, 169–171
archaeological objects, import restrictions on, 159–160
Art Dealers Association of America (ADAA), 49
art or artifacts. *See* cultural property
Arts and Cultural Affairs Law, New York, 11–12, 26, 27, 29, 31
attribution, warranty of, 23–32
auction, buying and selling art and collectibles at
  consigning to auction, 85–99
  public auction, buying at, 101–112
authenticity, warranty of, 23–32
Autocephalous Greek Orthodox Church v. Goldberg Feldman Arts, 46, 163
autodialers, 140
autographed collectibles, 28, 31, 37, 38

B

baby FTC Acts, 182
Balog v. Center Art Gallery – Hawaii, Inc., 20
Bank Secrecy Act, 197
barter transactions, 194–195
bidder registration and credit arrangements, 102–103
bidding, 103
Bitcoin, 33
blockchain technology, 32–34
breach of contract (rescission), 174
breach of warranty claims, statutes of limitations on, 18–20
browsewrap agreement, 120–121
Bureau of Consumer Protection, 55, 179
buybacks, 63–65, 96
buyer as reseller: warranties, 71–72
buyer's premium (BP), 88–89
  payment terms and, 108

C

CAfA. *See* Court of Arbitration for Art (CAfA)
California Civil Code
  § 986, 81, 82
  § 1739.7, 12§ 1739.7(a)(6), 38
  § 1739.7(b), 27
  § 1740, 38
  §§ 1742, 26
  § 1742(d), 39
  § 1744.7, 11, 29
California law
  Board of Equalization, 189
  certificates of authenticity, 12, 24, 26–28
  consumer protection, 177, 182
  disclaiming warranties, 14, 15
  distinction between opinion and warranty in purchases, 11–12

California law *(continued)*
  implied warranties, 12–13
  limited edition defined by, 38
  mandatory warranties, 15
  mint condition, attempt to codify definition of, 37
  resale royalty, 81–82
  review sites, 116
  statutes of limitations, 20
  Telephonic Sellers Law, 141
  use taxes, 189
Carter v. Helmsley-Spear, 80
Castillo v. G&M Realty, 80
catalogue sellers, 139
cataloguing, 91–93
CBP. *See* Customs and Border Protection (CBP)
certificates of authenticity, 11–12, 26–28
Certified Coin Exchange (CCE), 55, 119
Christie's, 19, 30, 32, 62–63, 82, 87, 96, 97, 106, 107, 110, 111
clickwrap agreement, 121–122
CMI. *See* copyright management information (CMI)
Code of Federal Regulations, 16 C.F.R. 255.5, 116
Coin Dealer Newsletter (CDN), 36, 58
coins
  arbitration in purchase of, 170
  buy-back policy, 64, 180
  buying at auction, 108
  buying online, 116–117, 119, 144
  consigning to auction, 87, 92
  copyright protection for design of, 129
  counterfeiting, 32
  as cultural property, 158–161
  dealers of, selling through, 73, 75
  disclaiming warranties on, 14–16
  Federal Trade Commission (FTC) and, 179–181
  in individual retirement accounts (IRAs), 195–196
  liquidity of, 60–63
  misrepresentations of, 52–53
  negotiating purchase of, 168
  past appreciation statistics on, 58–60
  pricing and overpricing, 54–58
  of the realm, 188
  recordkeeping requirements on sizeable purchases of, 196–197
  replica, Hobby Protection Act and, 177
  return privileges, when buying online, 144
  sales tax on price of, 187–188, 190–191, 193, 195–197
  as securities, 67–68
  statutes of limitation on breach of warranty claims, 19
  telemarketing, selling through, 137, 138, 141
  treasure coins, 32
  uncirculated or mint state designations, 13, 35
  in United States, illegal, 153–154
  warranties of condition, quality, grade, 35–36
  warranty of authenticity/attribution of, 25, 26, 29, 32
  warranty of rarity/surviving mintage, 38, 39–40
cold calls, 138–139
collector, qualifying, 191–193
commissions and other charges, 88–90
common law torts (damages), 174–176
condition, warranty of, 35–37
consigned goods, "voidable" title to, 46–49
consigning to auction, 85–99
  consignment agreement, 85–94
  estimates, 94–95
  guaranteed minimum prices, 96–97
  nonpayment by buyer, risk of, 98
  reserves, 95–96
  settlement: timing and procedure, 97
  summary of, 98–99
consignment agreement, 85–94
  advances, 90–91
  cataloguing, 91–93
  commissions and other charges, 88–90
  consignor's warranties, 93–94
  exclusive right to sell, 86
  timing and location of sale, 87–88
consignments to dealers, 72–73
consignor's warranties, 93–94

Convention on Cultural Property Implementation Act, 158
COPY notice, 155
Copyright Act, 82, 125–126, 173
Copyright Alternative in Small-Claims Enforcement Act (CASE Act), 172–174
Copyright Claims Officers, 173
copyright considerations when displaying art and collectibles online, 125–135
  accuracy of photo, 134
  collectables, 128
  copyright notice, 127–128
  descriptions, copyrighted, 134
  Digital Millennium Copyright Act (DMCA), 130–131, 173
  fair use issues with displaying artwork and data, 129–132
  length of copyright protection, 128
  non-fungible tokens (NFTs), 126–127
  numismatics and philately, 129
  ownership of copyrights, 125–129
  posting images of copyrighted items that are for sale: the "first sale rule," 132–134
  summary of, 135
  terms and conditions of websites items are shared on, 134
  works of art, 125–128
copyright disputes, 172–174
copyright management information (CMI), 130
counterfeit art or collectible items, 13, 15, 18, 26, 29, 32, 105–108, 127, 155
Court of Arbitration for Art (CAfA), 170
credit arrangements, for bidder, 102–103
Cristallina v. Christie's, 96
cultural property
  buying and importing, 157–164
  collections of ancient art and artifacts acquired by theft, 157–158
  definition of, 158
  designated lists of items subject to seizure and forfeiture, 160–162
  foreign country's export restrictions on any important work present within their boundaries, 163–164
  imported into United States prior to enactment of relevant laws, 163
  import restrictions on archaeological objects, 159–160
  international and domestic legislation regulating trade of, 158
  legality of owning, 158–159
  memorandums of understanding (MOUs), 160–161
  Native American art or artifacts, 162
  private actions against possessors of stolen or illegally exported, 162
Cultural Property Advisory Committee (CPAC), 160–161
Cultural Property Implementation Act (CPIA), 158–159, 161
currency replicas, 154–155
Customs and Border Protection (CBP), 159–161

D

damages (common law torts), 174–176
Dawson v. G. Malina, 28–29
dealers, buying and selling art and collectibles through
  additional considerations, 82
  express and implied warranties generally, 9–21
  for investment, 51–69
  moral rights, 79–80
  resale rights, 81–82
  selling art or collectibles through, 71–77
  title, getting good, 43–50
  warranties of authenticity, condition, and rarity, 23–41
  written contract, 3–8
dealers as fiduciaries, 65–66
descriptions, copyrighted, 134
designated lists of items subject to seizure and forfeiture, 160–162
differing remedies (statutory violations), 176–178
Digital Millennium Copyright Act (DMCA), 130–131, 173

Directive 2001/84/EC, 81
disclaimer of other warranties, 104–108
disclaiming warranties, 14–16
Disclosure of Material Connections rule, 116
discovery rules, 177–178
DIY auctions and sales, 117–119
Do Not Call Registries, 137, 140
droit de suite, 81
droit moral, 79–80

E

eBay, 59, 117–119, 131, 143, 148
electronic copyright protections, 130
entruster rule: protecting yourself, 73–76
ESIGN (Electronic Signatures in Global and National Commerce) Act, 5
estimates, 94–95
Ethereum, 33
exclusive right to sell, 73, 86
express and implied warranties
generally, 9–21
  disclaiming warranties, 14–16
  express warranties *versus* statements of opinions, 10–12
  implied warranties, 12–14
  mutual mistake, 16–17
  statutes of limitations on breach of warranty claims, 18–20
  summary of, 21

F

Facebook, Inc. v. Duguid, 140
fair use issues with displaying artwork and data, 129–132
Federal Arbitration Act, 173
Federal Trade Commission (FTC), 179–182
  baby FTC Acts, 182
  Bureau of Consumer Protection, 55, 179
  Disclosure of Material Connections rule, 116
  FTC Act § 5, 179–182
  Telemarketing and Consumer Fraud and Abuse Prevention Act, 138
  Telemarketing Sales Rule, 140, 176, 181
Feigen & Co. v. Weil, 72
fiduciaries, dealers as, 65–66
Financial Crimes Enforcement Network (FinCEN), 198
fine art, defined, 82
Firestone & Parson v. Union League of Philadelphia, 18
first sale doctrine, 132–133
first sale rule, 132–134
fitness for particular purpose, 14
floating reserve, 95–96, 97
floor bidding, 101–102
  perils of, 108–109
for-profit determination, 192, 193–194
FTC Act § 5, 179–182
FTC v. Security Rare Coin & Bullion Corp., 64, 180–181
FTC v. Solomon Trading Co., Inc., 56, 58, 59

G

Galin v. Hamada, 48
Gil v. Winn-Dixie Stores, Inc., 148–149
government property in United States, illegal, 153–154
grade, warranty of, 35–37
grey market art or collectible items, 32
guaranteed minimum prices, 96–97

H

Hagen v. J.I. Corporation, 19
Hahn v. Duveen, 30
HEAR Act, 46
Heritage Auctions (ha.com), 40, 47, 63, 87–88, 93, 104–105, 119, 130
Hobby Protection Act, 32, 154–155, 176, 177
Holdbrook Pediatric Dental, LLC, v. Pro Computer Service, LLC, 122
Hope v. Klabal, 175

I

illegal art or collectibles, 153–155
  currency replicas, 154–155
  summary of, 155
  United States coins and government property, 153–154
implied warranties, 12–14

income tax, 190–194
individual retirement accounts (IRAs), 116, 195–196, 199
Internal Revenue Code, 194
Internal Revenue Service (IRS)
art and collectibles in individual retirement accounts, 195, 196
barter transactions and, 195
Form 1099-B, 197
Form 8300, 197
for-profit determination, 192, 193–194
qualifying as collector or investor, 191–193
Regs. Sec. 1.183-2(b)(4), 193
Regs. Sec. 1.183-2(b)(7), 192
sales of art or collectibles seized by, 104
wash sales, 194
See also taxes
Internet bidding, 94, 102
Internet Protocol (IP), 198
investment, buying art and collectibles for, 51–69
buybacks and portfolio "updates," 63–65
dealers as fiduciaries, 65–66
liquidity, 60–63
materiality and reliance, 53–54
misrepresentation *versus* literal truth, 51–53
past appreciation statistics, 58–60
pricing/overpricing, 54–58
securities, art or collectible items as, 66–68
summary of, 69
investment advisors, 116
investment opportunities, 138
investor, qualifying, 191–193
IRC Sec. 183(d), 193

J
Jenack v. Rabizadeh, 5–6
Judicial Arbitration and Mediation Services (JAMS), 169

K
Kirtsaeng v. John Wiley & Sons, Inc., 133

L
Lanham Act, 32, 155, 176–177
ledger, 33
legislation regulating trade of cultural property, 158
like-kind exchanges, 194–195
limited editions, 26, 27, 34, 38–40, 57, 138
limited liability companies (LLCs), 196
liquidity, 60–63
literal truth, 51–53
litigation, 171–172
Llewellyn v. North American Trading, 68
loss in buying remotely, risk of, 143–144

M
mail bidding, 103
Martin Act, 68
Massachusetts Chapter 93A, 182
materiality, 53–54
Mechigian v. Art Capital Corp., 66
memorandums of understanding (MOUs), 160–161
mint condition, 13, 24, 35, 37
misrepresentation, 51–53
moral rights, 79–80, 82
mutual mistake, 16–17, 72

N
National Stolen Property Act, 159
Native American art or artifacts, 162
Native American Graves Protection and Repatriation Act (NAGPRA), 162
negotiation (working it out with the dealer), 167–169
New Mexico Cultural Properties Act, 162
New York Arts and Cultural Affairs Law
§ 11.01.20, 26, 27
§ 13.01, 11
§ 13.05, 29, 31
§ 60.02, 12
New York Department of Consumer Affairs, 110, 183
New York law, 15, 96, 175
Arts and Cultural Affairs Law, 11–12
attribution, distinctions relating to, 24
auction regulations, 97, 102, 110–111, 183

New York law *(continued)*
certificates of authenticity, 26–28
consignor's warranty, 93
consumer protection, 177, 182–183
disclaiming warranties, 14, 15
distinction between opinion and warranty in purchases, 11–12
Gen. Obl. Law § 5-701(a)(6), 5–6
implied warranties, 12–13
mandatory warranties, 15
statutes of limitations, 20
use taxes, 189
New York's auction regulations, 110–111, 183
Nguyen v. Barnes & Noble, Inc., 120–121
non-fungible tokens (NFTs), 32–34, 118, 126–127, 135
nonpayment by buyer, risk of, 98
Numismatic Guaranty Corporation (NGC), 14–15, 36

O

online agreements, enforceable, 119–122
online buying and selling of collectibles. *See* remotely buying and selling art and collectibles
online sales platforms, common practices for, 117–119
auction, 117
best offer, 118
buy it now, 117–118
DIY, 118–119
oral amendments to written agreements, 7–8
ownership of copyrights, 125–129

P

past appreciation statistics, 58–60
Patriot Act, 197
payment terms, buyer's, 108
pooling, 109–110
Porter v. Wertz, 48, 49
portfolio updates, 63–65
possessors of stolen or illegally exported, private actions against, 162
precious metals
buying online, 116
in individual retirement accounts (IRAs), 196
liquidity of, 60
recordkeeping requirements on sizeable purchases of, 197–198
selling through telemarketing, 137, 138, 141
Pre-Columbian Monument Act, 162
premium, buyer's, 108
pre-purchase inspections, 15–16
pricing/overpricing art and collectibles for investment, 54–58
private treaty sales, 86
Professional Coin Grading Service (PCGS), 14–15, 36, 40, 52
Professional Numismatists Guild (PNG), 32, 107, 117, 170–171
Professional Sports Authenticators (PSA), 37
protecting yourself: entruster rule, 73–76
provenance representations, 49
public auction, buying at, 101–112
absentee bidding, 103
bidder registration and credit arrangements, 102–103
buyer's premium and payment terms, 108
disclaimer of other warranties, 104–108
floor bidding, 101–102
perils of, 108–109
Internet bidding, 103
mail bidding, 103
New York's auction regulations, 110–111
pooling, 109–110
summary of, 111–112
warranty of title, 103–104
publicly displayed art, moral rights in, 82

Q

quality, warranty of, 35–37

R

rarity/surviving mintage, warranty of, 37–40
registration, of bidder, 102–103

reliance, 53–54
remedies, 174–178
  breach of contract (rescission), 174
  common law torts (damages), 174–176
  statutory violations (differing remedies), 176–178
remotely buying and selling art and collectibles, 115–123
  Americans with Disabilities Act (ADA) in, 147–149
  copyright considerations when displaying art and collectibles online, 125–135
  enforceable online agreements, 119–122
  online sales platforms, common practices for, 117–119
  return privileges in, 144–145
  review sites and, 116–117
  rights and risks in, 143–149
  risk of loss in, 143–144
  sales and use tax laws in, 145–147
  summary, 123
  telemarketing, 137–141
  24/7 access to information, 115–117
resale rights, 81–82
resale royalty, for buying or selling art outside of United States, 82
resale royalty law, 81–82
rescission (breach of contract), 174
reserves, 95–96
return privileges, in buying remotely, 144–145
review sites, 116–117
Rosen v. eBay, 133–134
Rosen v. Spanierman, 19–20, 175

S

safe harbor status, 131
sale, timing and location of, 87–88
sales tax, 187–188
  laws in buying remotely, 145–147
Sam Francis Foundation v. Christie's, Inc. et al., 82
SARs. *See* Suspicious Activity Reports (SARs)
securities, art or collectible items as, 66–68
Securities and Exchange Commission (SEC), 68
SEC v. Brigadoon Scotch Distributors, Ltd., 67–68
SEC v. W.J. Howey Co., 66–67
selling art or collectibles through dealers, 71–77
  buyer as reseller: warranties, 71–72
  consignments to dealers: terms and conditions, 72–73
  entruster rule: protecting yourself, 73–76
  summary of, 77
settlement: timing and procedure, 97
SGC of Boca Raton, 37
Sheldon Scale, 35
Sherman Antitrust Act, 109–110
Sherwood v. Walker, 16
signature requirement, 4–6
Sinclair v. Ziff Davis, 134
Sotheby's, 29, 30, 47, 62, 87, 94–95, 97, 106–107, 111
South Dakota statute, 146–147, 188, 189–190
South Dakota v. Wayfair, et al., 146, 188, 189–190
sports cards, 4, 13, 16, 30, 35–36, 37, 74, 194
sports memorabilia, 15, 27–28, 31, 36, 37, 177
stamps
  cataloguing, 91, 92
  consigning to auction, 87
  copyright protection for design of, 129
  counterfeiting, 32
  as cultural property, 158
  disclaiming warranties on, 16, 107–108
  liquidity of, 61
  past appreciation statistics on, 58
  pricing and overpricing, 56
  warranties of condition, quality, grade, 35
  warranty of authenticity/attribution of, 25
  warranty of rarity/surviving mintage, 38, 39

State Attorneys General, 182–183
statements of opinions, express warranties *versus,* 10–12
Statute of Frauds, 3–8
contract = offer + acceptance, 4
exceptions to, 8
oral amendments to written agreements, 7–8
quantity/price included in, 7
signature requirement, 4–6
statutes of limitations on breach of warranty claims, 18–20
statutory violations (differing remedies), 176–178
stolen items
National Stolen Property Act, 159
possessors of stolen, private actions against, 162
title to, 44–46
Suspicious Activity Reports (SARs), 197–198
Swift v. Zynga Game Network, Inc., 122

T

takedown notice procedures, 130
Tax Cut and Jobs Act, 194
taxes, 187–199
art and collectibles in individual retirement accounts, 195–196
in buying remotely, 145–147
income tax, 190–194
like-kind exchanges and barter transactions, 194–195
recordkeeping requirements imposed by the United States, 196–199
sales tax, 187–188
summary of, 199
use tax, 188–190
telemarketers
description of, 138–140
registration of, 138–140
requirements for, 140–141
telemarketing, 137–141
autodialers, 140
California's Telephonic Sellers Law, 141
catalogue sellers, 139
cold calls, 138–139
definition of, 138
Do Not Call Registries, 140
noncompliance, penalties for, 141
regulation of, 137
requirements of sales representative, 140–141
summary of, 141
Telemarketing and Consumer Fraud and Abuse Prevention Act, 138, 140, 144, 176, 181, 182
Telemarketing Sales Rule, 140, 176, 181
Telephone Consumer Protection Act (TCPA), 140
telephone sales. *See* telemarketing
Telephonic Sellers Law, California's, 141
terms and conditions, 72–73
Texas Deceptive Trade Practices-Consumer Protection Act, 177–178, 182
timing and location of sale, 87–88
title
getting good, 43–50
provenance representations, 49
to stolen items, 44–46
summary of, 49–50
voidable title to consigned goods, 46–49
warranty of, 43–44, 103–104
torts, 174–176

U

uncirculated, 13, 24, 35–36
UNESCO Convention, 158–159
UNIDROIT, 162
Uniform Commercial Code (UCC)
§ 2-201, 3–4
§ 2-209, 7
§ 2-312, 43
§ 2-313, 10–11
§ 2-314(2), 12–13
§ 2-314(3), 13
§ 2-315, 14
§ 2-316, 14–16
§ 2-403(1)(b), 47–48
§ 2-725, 18–19, 44, 175
auction sales, 104

authenticity problems, 107
contract price requirement, 7
exceptions to the Statute of Frauds, 8
signature requirement, 4–6
statute of limitations under, 19, 20, 168, 174, 175, 177–178
UCC-1 financing statement, 75–76
voidable title to consigned goods, 47–49
warranties, legal rules and principles applicable to, 9–21
warranties of title, 43–44
warranties when buyer is reseller, 71–72
United States
coins and government property, illegal, 153–154
counterfeiting coins and postage stamps, 32
Cultural Property Advisory Committee (CPAC), 160–161
Cultural Property Implementation Act (CPIA), 158–159, 161
cultural property imported into, prior to enactment of relevant laws, 163
Customs and Border Protection (CBP), 159–161
first sale doctrine, 132–133
Native American art or artifacts, protection of, 162
recordkeeping requirements imposed by, 196–199
United States v. Ronald Pook, 109–110
US Codes
15 U.S.C. § 6101, 138
15 U.S.C. § 7001, 5
17 U.S.C. § 106A, 38
17 U.S.C. § 109(a), 132–133
19 U.S.C. § 2606(c)(2)(A) and (B), 161
US Copyright Office, 125, 131, 133, 165
use tax, 188–190
use tax laws in buying remotely, 145–147

V

Visual Artists' Rights Act (VARA), 38, 80
visual art multiples, 26
voidable title to consigned goods, 46–49

W

warranties, 23–41
of authenticity/attribution, 23–32
blockchain technology and non-fungible tokens (NFTs), 32–34
buyer as reseller, 71–72
of condition, quality, grade, 35–37
consignor's, 93–94
disclaimer of other, 104–108
of rarity/surviving mintage, 37–40
summary, 40–41
of title, 43–44, 103–104
wash sales, 194
websites items are shared on, terms and conditions of, 134
wholesale value, 55–56, 64–65, 144
windfalls, 17
written agreements, oral amendments to, 7–8
written contract, 3–8
items included in, summary of, 8
Statute of Frauds, 3–8